The AUSTRALIAN Women's Weekly *Garden Guides*

Secret gardens

By Geoffrey Burnie

This is a book for gardeners who value their privacy and find relaxation and enjoyment in the natural surroundings they have created. The garden is their favourite part of their home; an inviting, secluded place. In this book we'll show you how to create your own secret garden. You'll see how to choose plants that are right for your area and how to put them together well. You'll find simple design concepts plus ideas for garden structures, ornaments, entrances, paths, and more. But please don't be distracted by the plants shown. If you can't grow them in your climate, there are countless others that you could use to create a similar effect.

Secret Gardens

The Discreet Charm of the Secret Garden

Throughout the world, behind high walls and fences, impenetrable hedges or dense shrubberies, lie countless hidden gardens. They are the creations of people to whom home is truly a haven. In their secret gardens they find respite from the city clamour and refreshment in the beauty and tranquillity of natural surroundings.

Apart from the outer edges of enclosing shrubberies or a glimpse of foliage above walls, these gardens are invisible. Their inner reaches are not for show; they are for the exclusive use and enjoyment of owners and guests. Certain of privacy, the owners are free to use them without the inhibiting feeling of being observed. Inside your home, you draw the curtains so that you can live privately. Outside, trees and shrubs, fences and walls can become the curtains to your garden.

But there's more to a secret garden than privacy; it has inner secrets as well. It's dense and enticing, not sparse with open lawns, and it can't be summed up in a single glance, it has to be explored and you'll want to explore it! You'll want to wander down its winding paths and discover its hidden charms.

You can create a secret garden regardless of the size, shape and location of your land. Sure, a small, walled, inner-city courtyard has ready- made privacy and intimacy, but even the largest garden can have secrets; there's room to grow banks of encircling shrubs, space for paths to meander and scope for secluded sun-traps and entertaining areas. It can be dense and mysterious; an alluring forest garden. Or you can create a garden within a garden, a small space concealed behind a shrubbery or hedge.

A wall away from the encircling city, yet a million miles from there. Block out the sight of the true surroundings and a garden can transport you anywhere.

Planning a garden is an opportunity to be creative; fill it with things you love. This fountain makes an artistic and elegant feature which suits the Victorian house and its courtyard.

Paths have pulling power. They draw your attention towards the garden and your feet follow. A path that disappears behind a bank of shrubs demands exploration.

The charm and intimacy of a private courtyard is created in a big garden by enclosing a small section. Here is a delightful small garden with a promise of more through the gate.

Getting Started on a Garden

Forget buying the plants, start with plans

Whatever the size of your land, if you want to turn it into the garden of your dreams, dream on; it's a beneficial part of the process.

Before you plant anything, try to visualise the finished, fully grown garden. You must know the look you want before you can buy and install the elements that will achieve it. You should also know what you want will work.

'See' the garden you want

The panel below details the steps you should take to become familiar with your site. When you have taken them, you can start to visualise your garden. You don't have to know anything about plants to do this. You needn't worry about what plant goes where at this stage; just concentrate on the overall impression of the garden. Envisage walls and floors of foliage and where they should go; imagine banks of foliage and empty spaces for paths and paved areas and how they are arranged. You are designing a space in which to live, using plants as the building blocks; ground covers for floors, shrubs for walls and trees

Get to Know your Site

The best way to decide what you want is to study the site

INSIDE THE HOUSE

- *Which rooms face the garden and is their view important?*
- *How much light enters and could trees or shrubs grow to obstruct it? How tall would they need to be to do this?*
- *Do you have privacy indoors? If the answer is no, could plants provide it?*

OUTSIDE THE HOUSE

- *How much space do you have?*
- *What do you already have; walls, fences, plants, paving, paths and so on?*
- *Which is the sunny side? (In the southern hemisphere it's the north; in the northern hemisphere it's the south).*
- *Is the sunny side obstructed by buildings or trees?*
- *Looking beyond your boundary, is there a view or outlook? Conversely, is there something you'd rather not see; could a tree or shrubs hide it?*
- *What's the soil like? Dig a few holes to a depth of 30cm (12in) and see what comes up; then fill the holes with water. If there's any water left after 24 hours you have a drainage problem and may need to install sub-surface pipes.*

for ceilings. The only complication is these building blocks are not their final size when you place them.

When you settle on a bank of foliage for a particular spot, imagine what its final height will be, then consider the effects of that height.

What width would such a plant or plants need and do you have the space?
How much shadow would be cast and where?
Walk around the garden and into the house. Would a planting of that height and width have any other effects?

Now consider the plants

After you know the size of the specimens and where they will be, you can decide on the plants you'd like to use. You are only limited by what is available, what will grow in your climate and on your site; that leaves hundreds, even thousands of possibilities.

Where do you start?

Try listing all the plants you would like to include; put them in categories like 'tree', 'big shrub', 'small shrub', 'groundcover', etc. If you know that they're deciduous or evergreen, note that too.

Learn from local experience

Another good idea is to take a notepad and pen and walk around the neighbourhood to see what grows well. Not everything will be in flower so look for size, shape, density of foliage, colour and texture of leaves and general good health.

Observe plant combinations and note how they grow together to form a mass. Note the space that mature plants take up.

If you see something you like but don't know its name, why not knock on the door? Gardeners are usually generous

DRAWING A PLAN ON PAPER

Is it necessary?

No! If you like drawing then go ahead; it's a good way to establish the number of plants of a size you'll need and whether your ideas are too grand for the space.

But remember, you will never see or use your garden in plan view, that is, from above. It is also hard to depict in plan the smaller plants that will grow beneath other, taller varieties.

Better to draw your garden ideas in perspective (from eye level). This is much harder to do and most of us can't manage it, but we can all visualise various design ideas in our minds.

New to Gardening?

How to create a good garden the first time

If you're about to start work on your first garden and know next to nothing about plants and their needs, a good strategy is to keep it simple.

Choose plants you know are successful in your area, those with a minimum of maintenance (visit a nursery for help here), and use them, either massed together to cover a big area or in groups repeated throughout the garden.

An enormous variety of plants is not essential; it's possible to create a good effect with half a dozen species or less.

It's best to leave the 'one of everything' style of garden to gardeners who have the time and skill to care for them. The greater the number of different plants you buy, the more you have to learn to place them correctly and look after them.

Once your simple garden is established, you can add more variety as your interest grows. If it doesn't, you'll still have a lovely garden and the time to enjoy it.

people and, if they can't help with the name, they may let you take a piece to a garden centre for identification. Don't forget to ask how old the plant is; it may be just a baby that will grow much bigger.

Learn from the experts

Botanic Gardens are a good place to see mature plants and gardening books are full of colour pictures. For every plant you add to your list, find out:

- *Its height and spread.*
- *Its natural home and the conditions in which it occurs.*
- *Its needs (sun, shade, water, drainage, temperatures tolerated).*
- *Its pruning needs.*
- *Its flowering season and colour.*
- *Does it have other decorative features? When?*
- *Is it deciduous or evergreen?*

If you take the trouble to find these things out you will be in control of the look of your garden and minimise the elimination of plants later.

The role of the garden centre

Nurseries are the logical place to find plants but don't rush into buying them. If you have an idea of the sizes and characteristics of the plants you want the nursery staff can guide you to some choices. Note the names of the choices for further research.

Don't believe plant labels, especially regarding size; they are notoriously unreliable.

Nurseries tend to stock plants that are in flower now and buying up big on one visit can result in a garden display that comes and goes all at once.

All native to sunny, seasonally dry climates, these herbs, including thyme, lavender and oregano, look perfect grouped together and are easily grown in the same conditions.

Working with Nature

Climate affects the way plants look and grow

Plants from a particular climate zone have evolved to suit the weather conditions experienced in that climate. They can have a similarity of leaf shape, size, colour or texture that often doesn't match plants from a different climate.

For example, shrubs that occur naturally in cool, moist European woods may not combine with those from dry Australian forests. The tough, small leaves of Mediterranean plants are a mismatch with the big, lush leaves of plants from wetter sub-tropical regions. Nature would never have produced such a combination and they look out of place.

Of course there are exceptions to this and the observant gardener will find them. But as a general proposition, if you choose plants from only one type of climate zone, then your garden will have a unified and credible look to it.

Plants from wet climates have softer, more lush looking and sometimes bigger leaves than dry climate plants. Grouped together, these plants make a convincing, soothing wet woodland.

If that climate zone is also your climate zone, the garden will be easier to maintain, too. The plants will expect the temperatures you experience and they'll want about the same amount of rain at the times of year you get it. You may not have to water the garden at all, but if you do, you won't have to worry about giving plant A enough water while keeping neighbouring plant B dry!

Plants that suit your climate will remain healthy while those from a different regime may be stressed by the change. This weakens them, making them more susceptible to attacks by pests and diseases.

Zones of similarity

The world's climate has been divided into zones of similarity, see pages 10/11. The division is based on the amount and distribution of rainfall and average monthly temperatures. The climate where you live is not unique. Other parts of the world, perhaps on

Aspect of a Garden

How shade moves in a garden during the day.

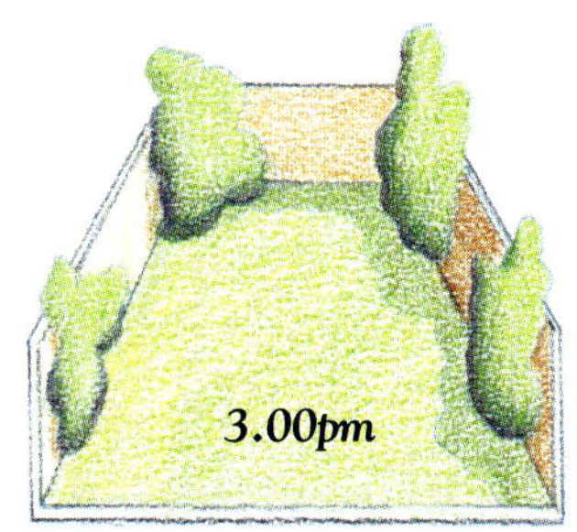

different continents, will have similar climates. Plants native to those areas can be good choices for your garden because they've evolved in a similar climate.

These zones are broadly, not narrowly, defined. A plant plucked from zone A in one part of the world, therefore, won't always thrive in the same zone in another part of the world. For example, the British Isles and the south-eastern corner of Australia are both considered rainy, maritime climates, but that part of Australia, although cool by local standards, has considerably warmer winters than the UK. Only plants from elevated parts have any chance of survival in an English garden. However, the zones share similarities and choosing plants from parts of the world that share your climate zone offers the best chance of success.

Sun vs shade

Aspect refers to the direction your garden faces in relation to the east-west path of the sun during the day. In the southern hemisphere the sun streams in from the north, in the northern hemisphere, south is the desirable sunny side.

If there is a building on your sunny side or you plant evergreen trees there, your garden will be shaded for some time either side of a mid-winter's day. The taller and closer the building or trees, the more months of the year you will be shaded.

To complicate matters, the position of the sun at noon, when it is at its highest, changes during the year from high overhead in mid-summer to quite low in the northern or southern sky in mid-winter.

This means that any buildings or trees on the sunny side will cast very long shadows in winter when you'd rather have the sun's free heat.

To maximise the sun's path through your garden, it's best to choose shrubs and plants that will grow to just the height you need in the sunny part of the garden. Also keep in mind that the further away a plant is from the spot where you want the sun, the taller you can have that plant.

How Shade Moves During The Year

In mid-summer, the sun at noon is as high overhead as it will ever be.

In mid-winter, noon sunlight streams in from a low angle; shadows are long, reducing light.

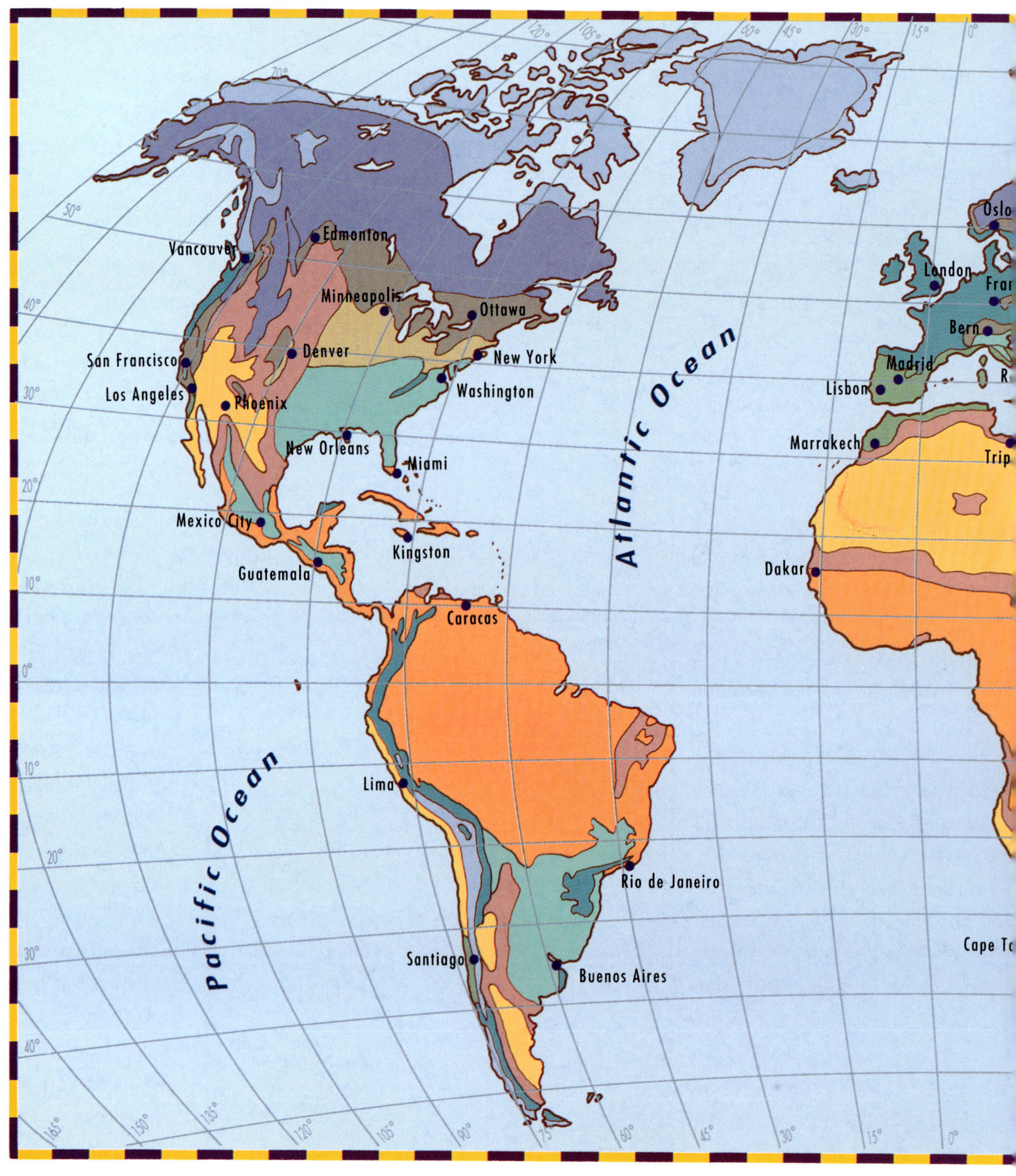

World Climate Zones

Use this map to locate areas of the world that have a climate similar to your own. Plants from those regions are most likely to be most successful in your garden.

Key to map

- *Tundra; average summer temperature 0°-10°C (32°-50°F). Very severe winters.*
- *Sub-Arctic; Severe winters. Average temperature above 10°C (50°F) for less than four months.*
- *Cold continental; rain year round or dry winters. Average summer temperatures below 22°C (72°F).*
- *Cool continental; severe winters but warm to hot summers. May be rainy year round or dry in winter.*
- *Temperate marine; cool winters, warm to hot summers. May be rainy year round or dry in winter.*

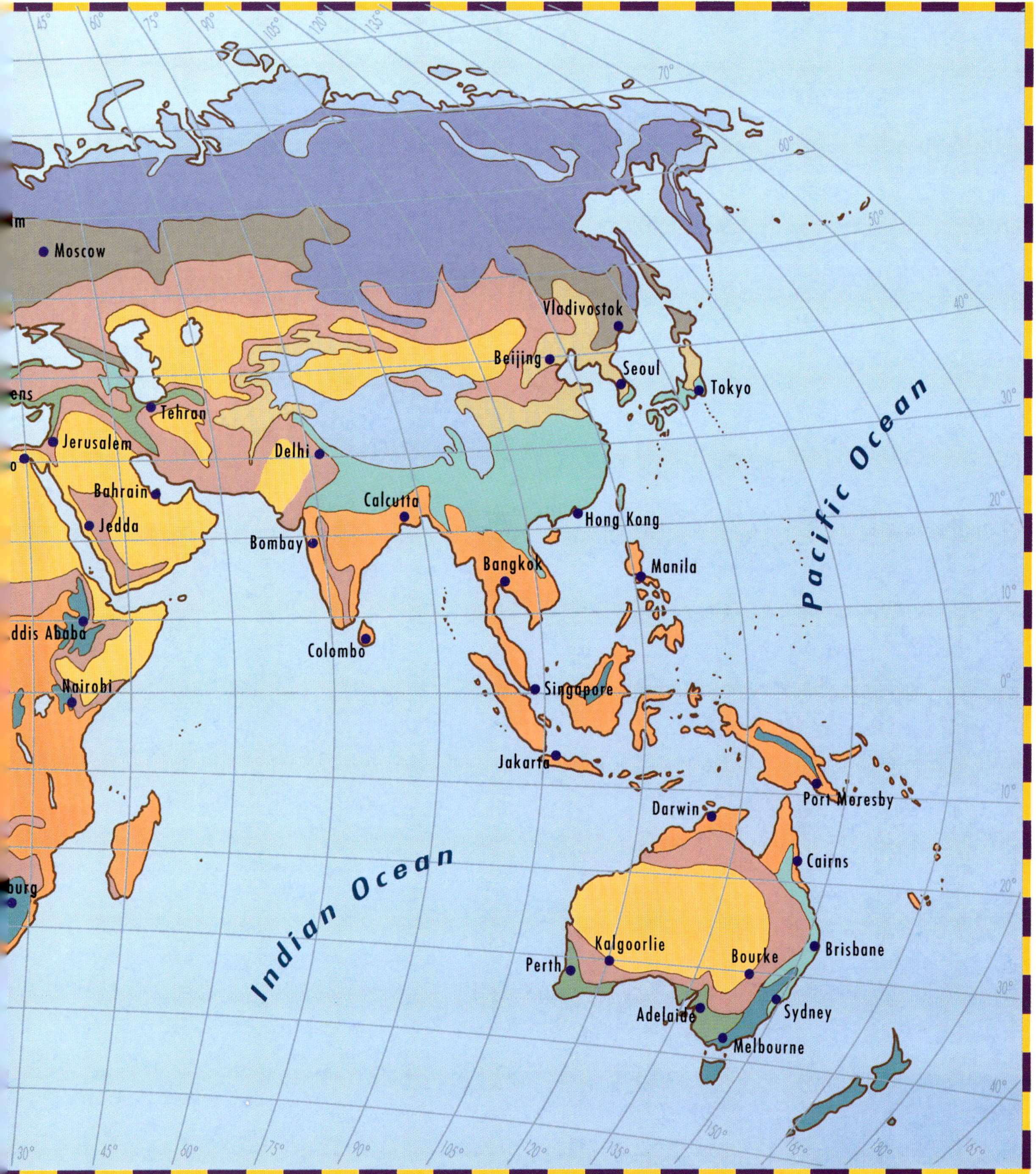

- *Subtropical; cool to mild winters, warm to hot summers. May be rainy year round or dry in winter.*
- *Mediterranean; cool to mild winters, warm to hot summers. Summers always dry.*
- *Semi-arid plains; relatively low rainfall which may be seasonal or evenly spread. Cold, cool or mild winters.*
- *Desert; very low rainfall. Winters may be cold or mild.*
- *Tropical; year round warmth above 18°C (64°F). High rainfall, heaviest in summer. Winters may be dry or less wet.*

Our terms defined

RAIN: *Includes snowfalls.*

COLD: *Where average temperatures in winter are always below 0°C (32°F).*

COOL: *Where average temperatures in winter are between 0°-7°C (32°-45°F).*

MILD: *Where average temperatures in winter are above 0°-7°C (32°F).*

WARM: *Where average temperatures in summer are below 20°C (68°F).*

HOT: *Where average temperatures in summer are above 20°C (68°F).*

Little Secrets

Courtyards, Secret by Design

Partially sheltered and already enclosed, courtyards just need filling. That's your job and it's one you'll love.

For a small outlay on some perennials, including Irises, Geraniums and larkspurs, a few shrubs and an ornamental urn, this gardener can enjoy this scene for years to come.

❖ *Creating a garden courtyard is fun and the results can be spectacular. The small size of a courtyard makes the creation cheaper; you can splash out on quality plants, materials and fittings because you won't be spending big on quantities. It's possible too, to do a lot of the small construction jobs, such as paving, yourself.*

❖ *Climate and aspect permitting, you can have the look you like, formal or informal, English cottage or Japanese garden, tropical forest or European woods, a meadow of flowers or a ferny glade, heathland, herb garden or American desert. Whatever landscape appeals to you, let it be your inspiration.*

A solid stone bench nestled in an informal mix of flowers, such as Nicotiana, alyssums and green Ixias, is all it takes to create a country cottage garden in just a few square metres.

❖ *Alternatively, your ideal courtyard could be a collection of favourite plants but be careful here; groupings of plants randomly chosen from a range of climate zones can look awkward together (see information on plant selection in "Working with Nature", page 7).*

❖ *Now we'll look at some courtyard styles and examine the ideas in each. Don't be distracted by the plants used; if they don't suit there are dozens that will.*

Peter Bateman/picture courtesy of House & Garden

Barely bigger than a light well, yet this space, brimming with newly planted flowers, including stocks, carnations, Chrysanthemums and Petunias, is both a pleasure to be in and to look down on.

DESIGN TIP

A good balance between empty spaces and masses of foliage is important. Space not only gives you freedom of access, it helps define the shape of the garden and leads the eye through it.

Above: Flowers popping up in cracks and crevices give a rustic, untamed look but don't let it go too far. When you start to lose sight of the paving, it's time to clear the lot away. New growth will appear next spring.

Leigh Clapp

Cottage Gardens In Courtyards

Recreating a Field of Flowers

You'll need full sun most of the day if you want to create an English cottage garden in your courtyard. Other essential elements include an exuberant mix of flowers in a not-too-tidy arrangement. Cottage gardens have a rather unkempt style, unlike the flower beds seen in parks. You can throw in some herbs and vegetables too and it's a good idea to keep track of the colour combinations you are creating.

Although small, you can wander through these courtyards. The one below left is a rectangular field of flowers bisected by an informal track that runs roughly down the centre. The eye is led down the path and straight to an object of interest, a chair, although it could have been a statue, fountain, sculpture or the like.

Confronted with this scene, few could resist being drawn down the path towards the destination. Along the way, there are plenty of distractions in the form of flowers and fragrances.

In the courtyard at far left a bank of bushy shrubs creates a sense of privacy and intimacy. It also helps shelter the garden and, being densely foliaged, attracts small birds.

Much of the courtyard floor is paved but the effect is softened by allowing plants to grow between the paving stones and in squares left unpaved for that purpose. However, don't give too much space to plants or you will lose the comfortable use of your garden. Here, overgrowth has made sitting at the table impractical.

Left:* *The exuberance of this small garden is created with a mix of many annual and perennial flowers that stay small, such as Aquilegias, Alchemillas and poppies, to give a good, long-lasting display of colour.

A GARDEN IN REVIEW

Turning Japanese

The site is shady. The style is Japanese. The result is a restful, contemplative garden.

Not facing the sun and shaded by the house and trees, this tiny courtyard is shady most of the day, most of the year. It could never support a colourful mix of sun lovers but is a good site for a forest floor garden. There's a Japanese theme to the design, although the garden could equally suggest a wood with a stream, a fern-filled glen, a rainforest or the shady, boggy margins of a lake.

What makes it a secret garden is its small size – 4x4m (13x13ft) – and the height and closeness of its walls. There are no buildings in sight and the tree that belongs to a neighbouring garden enhances the scene, implying that this is a hidden spot in a forest.

Plantings are simple, in the Japanese tradition; less than a dozen types of plants are used. Ornaments and a lantern reinforce the oriental theme but the fence introduces a local variation. Instead of traditional bamboo, it's brushwood of an Australian native shrub.

THE GARDEN IN BRIEF

- *Minimal sun dictates use of shade lovers.*
- *Choice of style: This gardener chose a Japanese theme but there are many alternatives.*
- *Size: It is too small to stroll through, too small for banks of shrubs or even one tree.*
- *Openness and small plants maximise apparent size of garden, reduce gloom.*

PLANTS USED

Groundcovers

1 *Australian violet (Viola hederacea)*

2 *Clubmoss (Selaginella apoda)*

Perennials

3 *Spathiphyllum candidum*

Shrubs

4 *Papyrus (Cyperus alternifolius)*

5 *Sacred bamboo (Nandina domestica & N.d. Nana)*

6 *Camellia sasanqua*

Climbers

7 *Pandorea pandorana*

ALTERNATIVES FOR COLD CLIMATES

Groundcovers

1 *Periwinkle (Vinca minor)*

2 *Bugleweed (Ajuga reptans)*

Perenials

3 *Hosta varieties*

Shrubs

4 *Oregon grape (Mahonia aquifolium)*

5 *Pieris japonica*

6 *Rhododendron*

Climbers

7 *Hydrangea petiolaris*

Warwick Kent

Paved Courtyards

Different Approaches to Container Gardening

Above: If you have more paving then you need, you can shape the space, and create more garden by grouping big pots together. Here a perimeter planting of shrubs is joined by a mixture of flowers in grouped containers.

Some courtyards are entirely paved, with gardening only possible in pots. While this restricts you to small-scale plants, it is still possible to soften the hard surfaces with a lush, dense planting.

If you have a paved courtyard you can still have a very attractive garden if you choose pots and their plants carefully. A collection of any old pots in every size and shape rarely looks good. Better to first decide on the look of the garden you want, then choose pots of a size and shape to suit the desired plants. If you want a lush look, choose big pots. The volume of soil they contain helps conserve water and, if small-growing plants are used, you can plant several in the one container.

Alternatively, you could turn a paved, walled courtyard into a desert landscape of stiff, stark plants. The advantage of plants from dry climates is that they usually cope if you forget to water. And, as they need less water in the first place, your paving is less likely to become damp and slippery.

Painted and paved in the colours of the desert, this sunny courtyard houses a cactus collection. The style, with its strong lines well displayed against sandy walls, is too restrictive for some, suiting a cactus collector or someone looking for an easy care garden with a distinctive look.

TIPS FOR SUCCESS WITH POTS

- *Where possible, avoid too many little pots – they dry out fast and plants soon become pot-bound.*
- *For a unified appearance, standardise the look of your pots. They don't have to be identical (though this can look good), just similar shapes and materials.*
- *Grouping pots together generally makes a more impressive display and they're a lot easier to water. However, in a formal layout you may need to place them at spaced intervals.*
- *Don't put small plants in very big pots. They'll look out of scale and never use all the soil available.*
- *Terracotta, earthenware and some concrete pots are porous whereas glazed ceramic, metal and plastic containers are not. The latter three will not dry out as fast and need less watering. Depending on the plants they contain and whether they're in sun or shade, the former group may need daily watering in summer. Watering washes nutrients out of the potting mix so plants in these containers will need frequent feeding. It's a good idea to feel down into the soil before watering; if it feels moist, don't water.*
- *Over time, potting mix in containers can become water repellant. Even after quite long soakings, the soil beneath the surface can remain dry. To check this, scratch the surface after watering. If the soil is dry, apply a wetting agent (from nurseries). Read the directions first and follow them strictly as these products are toxic to plants if applied in excess.*

Lorna Rose

Right: A wetter, greener part of the world inspired this courtyard. A triple row of pots, each progressively raised, lines the fenceline, forming a hillside of greenery. Deciduous grapevines on taut wires span the narrow space above, creating a cool, summer grotto beneath. Camellias, azaleas, Daphnes, Fuchsias and Gardenias thrive in the mild, moist conditions.

Left: Terracotta pots look stylish and colourful and there's a big range of shapes and styles to choose from. One disadvantage of terracotta is that its porous nature can lead to rapid drying out of the potting mix but that's not a problem when you use cacti or succulents such as these moonstones and Aloe vera. They'll live to forgive you if you forget to water.

Designer: Garth Phillips

Left: In a bright but partially shaded courtyard, wide terracotta dishes featuring a variety of shallow rooted annual flowers – Chrysanthemum, Impatiens, Lobelia and Petunia – give a good show of colour. Bigger, deeper pots house more substantial shrubs such as Camellia, Gardenia and cut-leaf maple.

Plants used:

1. *Archontophoenix cunninghamiana* (Bangalow palm)
2. *Dicksonia antarctica* (tree fern)
3. *Phoenix roebelinii* (pygmy date palm)
4. *Ficus benjamina* (weeping fig)
5. *Gardenia augusta*

THE TROPICAL LOOK FOR COOLER CLIMATES

Plants from tropical and sub-tropical areas look different to those from colder climates. They are evergreen and often have pointy, thick, large leaves.

While it's not possible to grow sub-tropical species in cold climates, you can create a similar look with plants that have the size and lushness of the warmer climate species.

Cool-climate ferns such as Osmunda and sword fern (*Polystichum spp.*) look as convincing as those from the tropics and Hosta, Bergenia and Solomon's seal have lush, tropical leaves. There's even a suitable palm: *Trachycarpus fortunei*, or the Chinese windmill palm, will tolerate winter lows of -12°C (10°F) in short bursts.

Warwick Kent

A GARDEN IN REVIEW

Illusion of Space

Although massing foliage in front of a wall decreases the area of usable space in a courtyard, it can create the opposite impression. When surrounding walls are hidden from view, the sense of being artificially enclosed vanishes. Instead of a tiny, inner city garden, this becomes a clearing in a tropical forest.

The tops of trees and shrubs visible in neighbouring gardens add to the impression of endless space as they seem the logical background to this garden.

Potted plants have several roles here. They add to the lush, tropical look and overall fullness of the garden, they help hide a wall and, because they are not lined up in a single row, they give an impression of depth. The pots themselves have a similarity of shape and style and look like a planned feature, not an afterthought. Should extra seating be required, the pots can be removed and cushions placed on the raised brick platform.

THE GARDEN IN BRIEF

- *Small rectangular area enclosed by high walls. Most groundspace is given to paving.*
- *Dense planting and neighbouring trees make the courtyard appear bigger.*
- *Gardening skill needed is minimal as is maintenance thanks to a simple, repetitive planting of only a few varieties.*
- *Plants chosen suit a frost-free climate.*

Pocket-sized Secrets

Ideas for Tiny Spaces

Your secret garden may be little more than a light well, a narrow side passage or a tiny porch but don't give up on it. Even small spaces become rewarding little gardens when you explore every possibility for places for plants. If you concentrate on small-growing plants, you can create an unusual garden of great variety.

Pots, troughs and window boxes are the obvious choices with which to create a garden in a bare patch with no soil, but don't forget the walls. As well as half baskets spilling over with greenery, walls can support climbers and decorative features such as latticework or ornaments. You may even find you can expand the garden by hanging a basket or two from an overhead support. Be careful here as hanging baskets will swing in the wind and are only suitable in areas that are sheltered.

When hanging pots, remember the supports must be strong enough to bear the wetted weight of the contents of the baskets.

Where there's no soil determined gardeners turn to pots, and if ground space is limited too, they hang them off the walls.

Lorna Rose

Lorna Rose

NARROW-GARDEN NOTES

Take care with narrow walkways; remember that first and foremost they are walkways. Don't plant something spiny or anything which will spread out over the path; you won't want to push your way through wet branches on a cold and rainy day. In the garden shown at right, the standard azaleas will never cause such a problem as they must be clipped regularly to preserve their globular heads. Other shrubs can be pruned back, but if you choose a species that won't spread much wider than the space you have, you'll minimise this task.

Above: One big specimen often has more impact than a cluster of lesser ones, especially if it is strong and striking in shape. This is sold as Dracaena marginata*, a popular indoor plant that's happier outside when frosts have finished. Give it a big pot, though, to avoid it looking top heavy. A wide, shallow dish is best.*

Lorna Rose

Leftt: Turning a long, narrow, mostly shaded passageway into an interesting garden presents several design challenges. This gardener chose to shorten the area's apparent length by dividing it into three spaces, each separated by lattice screens; the need for a walkway dictated narrow in-line planting. The central space is roofed for ferns and other shade lovers. In this first, open section, rather than force a natural style planting on an unnatural shape, a formal plan has been adopted. Visual interest has been created with a wall-mounted lattice frame flanked by clipped azaleas.

It's amazing what you can squeeze into a tiny space. This U-shaped alcove is made more private and green with a partial screen of shrubs across the open end. A little pergola adds to the enclosure and provides a home for a climbing rose (which in turn shades and shelters the seat). A lattice trellis, just visible at left, supports a shade-loving vine and clusters of pots around the bases of the walls supply ground level colour and interest – all this in about four square metres!

Lorna Rose

WALLPOTS AND BASKETS

Consider these points first:

- *Pots and their contents can be heavy, especially after watering. Ensure that supports are strong enough to bear the wetted weight.*
- *Walls that face the sun absorb and reflect a lot of heat. Small and/or porous pots will dry out very fast. Use the biggest containers you can, and safely secure and line the sides (but not the bases) with plastic to conserve soil moisture.*
- *Wire baskets lined with sphagnum moss or a fibre liner are prone to dry out in the shade or sun. These baskets can also be lined with plastic if drainage holes are pierced.*
- *Consider the hanging height of pots or baskets before deciding on contents. Fill those above eye-level with cascading plants, keeping low, compact varieties for pots or baskets at or below eye-level.*
- *If garden is exposed, remember hanging baskets will swing in the wind.*

GROWING PROBLEM

Avoid this mistake

Be cautious in your choice and positioning of trees. Planted in this tiny courtyard is a fiddle-leaf fig, 12m (40ft), Norfolk Island pine, 60m (200ft) and Chinese belltree, 12m (40ft). They look lovely together and form a dense screen but in a few years they will dominate this and the neighbour's courtyard. Sooner or later they will have to be removed, and the later the more difficult, dangerous and expensive the job. Know the ultimate height and spread of a tree or shrub and then site and space it accordingly.

Trees in Courtyards

Don't Plant a Potential Problem

Most trees are too big for courtyards as they can look out of scale and dominate the landscape. They cast shade over most or all of the ground space, restricting the plants you can grow to shade-lovers and making the courtyard and adjacent rooms gloomy. They also cast shade on at least one neighbouring property and this can lead to bitter disputes. Happily, there are some quite small trees that suit courtyards of moderate size and a selection of these is listed at right, but a better alternative may be to use big shrubs.

Many of these can be pruned into the shape of a small tree. The best bets are shrubs that grow 3-5m (10-16ft) tall on a single trunk although those with a few large trunks may also be trained into a thicket of small trees. Of course, shrubs that produce many thin stems such as Abelia and Forsythia can't be treated like this.

How To Turn a Shrub into a Tree

A technique for tiny gardens when even a small tree may be too big

Jeff Kilpatrick

This Cotoneaster has been trained into a small, attractive tree and a highlight of the courtyard. Left unpruned, Cotoneasters have low, wide-spreading branches but they can be trained into shape by removing the lower branches as the plant grows. This produces an umbrella-like canopy and a clean trunk or trunks.

Some other shrubs that can be converted into small trees include Tibouchina, Viburnum, Pieris, Osmanthus, Camellia, Cotinus, , Rhododendron, lilac and poinsettia.

Consider These Small Trees

Maples
(various species)

For cold and cool-temperate areas. There are several compact maples suitable for small gardens, including the Japanese, vine and Amur maple. All are deciduous and will tolerate winter lows of at least -20°C (-4°F).*

Redbud
(Cercis canadensis)

*7x7m (24x24ft)
For cool-temperate areas. Native to the eastern USA and Canada, this deciduous tree produces masses of pink flowers on bare stems in spring. It must have good drainage and may be single or multi-stemmed. Accepts -12°C (10°F)*.*

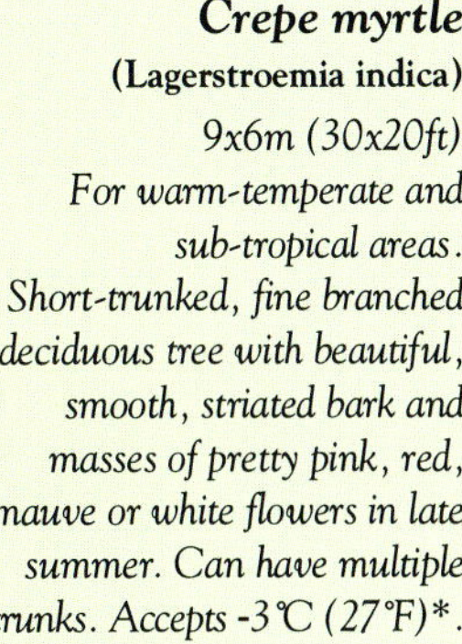

Crepe myrtle
(Lagerstroemia indica)

*9x6m (30x20ft)
For warm-temperate and sub-tropical areas. Short-trunked, fine branched deciduous tree with beautiful, smooth, striated bark and masses of pretty pink, red, mauve or white flowers in late summer. Can have multiple trunks. Accepts -3°C (27°F)*.*

Frangipani
(Plumeria rubra)

*5x5m (16x16ft)
For warm-temperate, sub-tropical and tropical areas only. One of the best small trees, the umbrella-shaped frangipani casts deep shade and has sweet, fragrant flowers all summer long. Leafless from mid-winter to late spring. Accepts 2°C (36°F)*.*

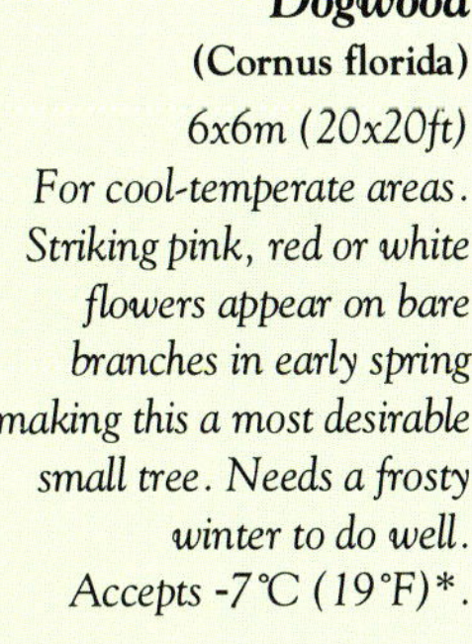

Dogwood
(Cornus florida)

*6x6m (20x20ft)
For cool-temperate areas. Striking pink, red or white flowers appear on bare branches in early spring making this a most desirable small tree. Needs a frosty winter to do well. Accepts -7°C (19°F)*.*

Chinese tallow
(Sapium sebiferum)

*12x6m (40x20ft)
but usually less.
For warm-temperate and sub-tropical areas. A deciduous tree, capable of good autumn tones even in mild areas. Ultimate size varies with climate and conditions and tree can be pruned if a lower canopy is desired. Accepts -3°C (27°F)*.*

****Temperatures tolerated are average minimums.
Plants will tolerate even lower temperatures for short periods (a day or two at a time).***

The Built Alternative

If you love the idea of lunch in the garden, an area of deep shade is essential for comfort and safety in summer. Trees are the logical choice where space permits but some gardens are too small for a tree and in such situations a pergola may be the solution. Pergolas can be covered with vines to cast a good, usable area of shade and, because vines grow faster than trees or large shrubs, you can be sitting in the shade within two or three summers instead of six or seven. In the first couple of years you can shade yourself by slinging canvas between the overhead beams or use split cane bamboo blinds.

Ways to Use Courtyard Walls

THREE WAYS TO CREATE A SOFTER, PRETTIER LOOK

Maximise the garden's growing potential and create a softer, prettier look by hiding bare walls behind a curtain of colour.

Climbers are the easiest way to cover a wall with greenery but there are other methods. You can espalier shrubs or trees against it. This involves training and pruning the plant into a flat, two-dimensional shape and is a useful and attractive way to grow fruit trees in small spaces.

A third alternative available to owners of dry stone walls is to grow small plants in pockets of soil between the blocks of stone that make up the wall.

The wall as a garden

Growing small plants in dry stone walls

If you have a dry stone wall, that is one built without mortar between the joints, it's possible to grow a big variety of interesting plants in between the stones. They'll be small plants as root space is restricted and you'll first have to pack soil into gaps in the wall.

Leigh Clapp

As a dry stone wall is attractive in its own right, you won't want to hide it, just enhance it. Small plants, such as the Campanula shown here, do just that. Other good choices include wallflowers (of course), Lewisia and varieties of Sedum, Saxifraga and Sempervivum.

CLIMBERS

Four ways to climb

1. Twining stems which spiral their way up a support. Examples include Carolina jasmine, honeysuckle, star jasmine and Wisteria.

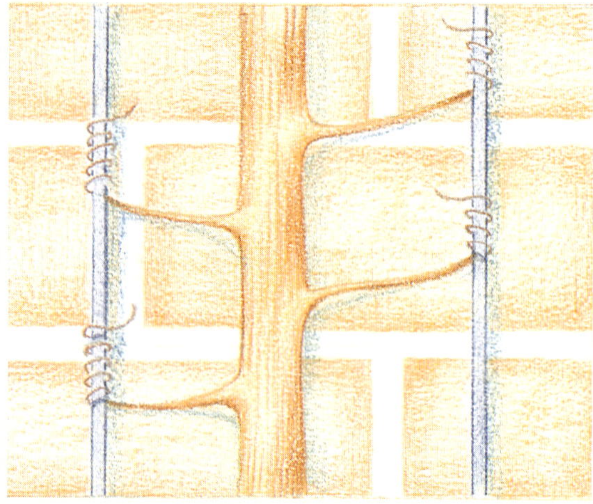

2. Tendrils on stems or leaf tips which twist firmly around nearby supports. Examples include Cissus, Antigonon, passionfruit and sweet pea.

3. Self-clinging aerial roots or pads which clamp the climber's stems onto even the smoothest vertical surfaces. Examples include English ivy, Virginia creeper, climbing fig and Euonymus fortunei.

4. Thorns or hooks which allow the climber to scramble over other shrubs or up into trees. The thorns point backwards to assist upward growth. Examples include Bougainvillea and climbing roses.

All climbers, apart from self-clinging ones, need support on which to climb a vertical surface. Many climbers live a long time and become heavy so the support must be durable and strong.

Climbers need training

All plants need light to live and, when the soil surface is crowded with competing plants, one way to get more light is to grow taller. Trees and shrubs construct woody frameworks to hold their leaves above competitors but climbers have developed a short cut up. They don't spend energy building scaffolding, they borrow someone else's!

A climber lives to climb. Their usual habit is to race straight up a support, forming a billowing mass at the top with little to cover the wall below.

But that's not what everyone wants. If you'd rather an even mass of foliage over the wall, you can train your climber from the start. Training involves directing the growing stems along the base of the support. When each end is reached, allow the stems to grow up a short distance then resume the horizontal training.

This is fiddly work but you end up with an even framework of stems to which the plant can be cut back when pruning becomes necessary – usually annually with climbers.

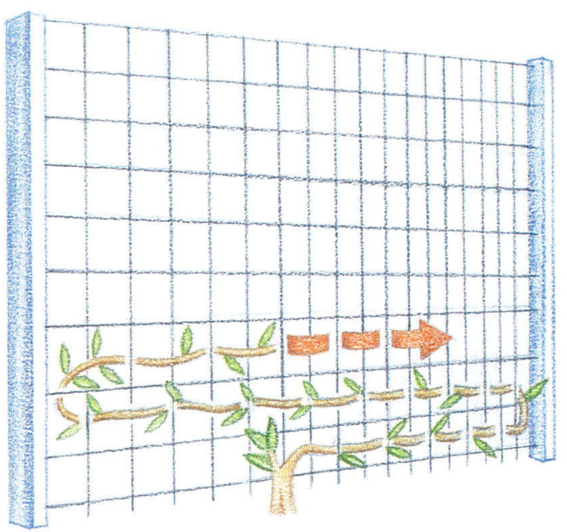

For even growth, train climbers from an early age, weaving stems back and forth until trellis is covered.

MAINTENANCE NOTES

Many climbers are extremely rampant and can get out of control, especially if space is restricted. Even the most vigorous vine can be kept to its allotted space with pruning, but pruning is time-consuming and may need to be undertaken several times a year in a small garden. You then need to dispose of the bulky prunings. If you don't have the time or inclination for this, be careful in your choice of climbers; keep in mind the space you have to cover and select those that stay small in your area.

Left alone, climbers head straight for the top of their support, leaving little or no cover below.

Two Climbers Better Than One?

It's possible to grow two, even three climbers together on the one wall. This can result in a tapestry-like foliage effect and a succession of flowers. Choose lightweight, small scale climbers or you will be pruning frequently to control rampant growth or stop one vine from swamping the other.

Boston ivy and related Virginia creeper are among the best self-clinging vines. Both are deciduous and the leaves colour well in autumn, even in frost-free areas. However both are rampant growers.

***Below:* Self-clinging Boston ivy (*Parthenocissus tricuspidata*) dominates its wall although the newly planted Wisteria is beginning to make inroads. Be aware Wisteria grown against a wall becomes quite heavy with age.**

Ivy Hansen

Above: Both Virginia creeper and related Boston ivy (shown) produce good autumn colour, even in frost-free climates. This effect was seen in Sydney where overnight temperatures in autumn might fall to 11°C (52°F). Self-clinging vines and vigorous growers, both of these climbers usually need annual pruning to keep them within bounds.

Some Lightweight Climbers

A selection of species for small spaces

These species are easily confined to small spaces with light pruning only. In warmer climates, those recommended for cold or mild areas usually become more vigorous. Temperatures given are minimums tolerated.

FOR COLD CLIMATES

***Clematis alpina* (-18°C or 0°F)**

***Parthenocissus henryana* (-18°C or 0°F)**

***Tropaeolum tuberosum* (-10°C or 14°F)**

FOR MILD CLIMATES

***Gelsemium sempervirens* (0°C or 32°F)**

***Hibbertia scandens* (-2°C or 28°F)**

***Lapageria rosea* (0°C or 32°F)**

FOR WARM CLIMATES

***Clerodendrum thomsoniae* (3°C or 37°F)**

***Asarina barclaiana* (0°C or 32°F)**

***Manettia bicolor* (5°C or 41°F)**

OTHER CHOICES FOR SMALL SPACES

By nature, climbers tend to be vigorous and in small spaces their use can create a maintenance headache.

You can minimise pruning tasks with careful plant selection. There are light-weight, less vigorous climbers and these should be sought when space is restricted.

Alternatively, some lax, normally trailing or ground-covering shrubs, such as Fuchsia, can be trained up a vertical support with no danger of unwanted, rampant growth.

The Fuchsia shown is the hybrid called "Sunray", a bushy, upright grower. With its main stems tied at intervals to a trellis, its trailing side branches hang down in overlapping tiers. Only where summers are cool can a Fuchsia grow against a sunny brick wall and even there, an east-facing aspect is best.

Espalier

Training shrubs to grow flat against a wall

Espalier is the art of training plants to grow in two dimensions, usually flat against a wall. The technique was developed centuries ago to allow a large number of fruit trees to be grown in a small space. Today, purely ornamental trees and shrubs are espaliered as the effect is novel and decorative.

Espalier involves retaining those branches which lie in the same plane as the wall against which they grow. All those that either grow towards the wall or away from it are removed. This produces a flat, two-dimensional result.

The retained branches can be allowed to grow naturally or tied to a geometric framework of battens or wires which produces a distinct pattern of growth. Successful espalier demands small amounts of regular attention to remove unwanted lateral growths and to tie retained branches early into desired positions.

Espaliers don't have to be grown against walls but if they are to be free-standing, some framework is necessary onto which to train the branches. Espalier is a skill and there are books which detail the steps to success which you can consult if you are interested in this ancient garden art.

Designer: Isabelle Greene

Above: Espaliered figs enhance the small space and a plain wall beside a pathway. Apart from the removal of certain lateral branches, these figs have been allowed to grow naturally, a relatively easy form of espalier but not as structured as one of the traditional geometric patterns.

Some Espalier Patterns

Belgian fence

Triple horizontal cordon

Palmette verrier

Triple vertical U-shape

Six grid

Fan

Single U

Double cordon

Feather

Single oblique cordon

STEP-OVER ESPALIERS

A useful idea for gardeners who like to grow a big range of fruit at home is the step-over espalier. These are low cordons, sometimes used as 'fences' around home orchards. Apples on dwarfing rootstocks are usually used and the plants are trained horizontally once they reach a height of about 25cm (10in). The single branch either side of the main trunk is trained along a taut wire which is attached to a stout stake up to 2m (6ft) from the trunk. Longer branches are possible but you should support them with additional stakes at intervals.

One reason to espalier fruit trees is to reduce fruit production. Most households can't use the quantities offered by mature trees but there's no problem consuming the moderate production of this espaliered apple tree. The simple T-shape is easy to train and maintain, takes up little garden space and causes minimal shading of the bed below.

A GARDEN IN REVIEW

Tiny Townhouse Transformed

Private, intimate and densely packed, this tiny, U-shaped area supports a secret city garden we'd all love to come home to. Close the gate behind you and you're in a different world. Here you can cast off stress and take in the beauty of the landscape you have created. There's something of interest everywhere and the richness of the scene suggests the wild beauty of a natural place. You wouldn't find the same sense of escape, freedom and adventure in a sparse, open, lawn garden.

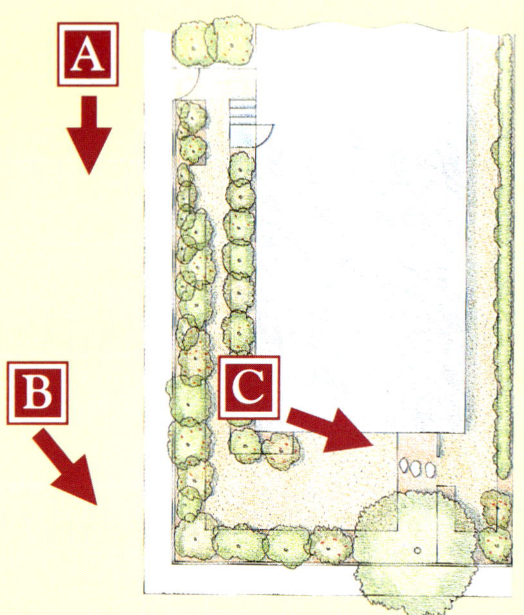

Situated on a corner, the garden encloses the house on three sides. The arrows indicate the position from which the pictures were taken.

Just two years old, this garden has been over planted to give it a full look quickly and the garden is at its peak now. It is bursting with beauty and interest, however, all these varieties cannot grow to maturity as there isn't the space for them. Hard pruning will control some, transplanting will better position others and others will still have to be removed to make way for new varieties or to keep paths and open areas clear.

Over-planting is a common mistake as gardeners always want to grow more varieties than they have space. While the plants are young and small they can be squeezed in and the garden looks fabulous in the first two years but, unless you are willing to prune hard and remove less favoured specimens as the garden grows, it will soon look overgrown and all plants will suffer as they compete for space, light, soil and water. In doing so, spindly growth and unattractive shapes will result.

Secret garden revealed

Situated on a corner, the garden forms a U around the house. The arm of the U which runs along the front of the house is about 3m (10ft) wide while that at the back is less than 2m (6ft) wide. The base of the U, which contains a paved area, has a depth of about 5m (16ft). The sunny side of the garden, yet well-shaded by a blue spruce tree and many shrubs, is a perfect spot for a lunch or brunch.

Outside, the street is wide and open with few trees, but step inside the gate and the contrast couldn't be greater. Suddenly the environment is bushy and beautiful. Your eye goes straight to the path. It's not clear where it leads but its overgrown appearance stirs your curiosity. You want to see what's beyond; you are drawn by intriguing glimpses of the interior.

THE GARDEN IN BRIEF

- *Density and variety of planting is interesting and surprising given the open streetscape. However, this has been achieved by over-planting and, as growth continues, some plants will have to go.*

- *Path creates a long vista, leading the eye and then drawing the feet into the garden.*

- *Path has visual interest. It includes two steps although the garden is flat and, beyond the first step, it widens suddenly into a small viewing bay.*

- *Path is as narrow as it can be. Note the encroachment of the groundcovers at the first step. They impede easy access and, being sunlovers, will become weak and spindly with the increasing shade of the Rhododendron at right. Many of the plants here will suffer that fate as the garden grows.*

Make your way down the path and you come to a clearing, the main part of the garden at the base of the U. It's a private, paved area on the sunny side, big enough for a table and a delightful setting for a long summer lunch. Here, too, there's an astonishing variety of plants, all intermingling into solid banks of colour and interest.

❶ *The clearing is a logical destination for the path and its relative openness makes a pleasing contrast to the closeness of foliage just passed through.*

❷ *There's a lot of foliage to see and a hint of more to come through this gate at the rear.*

❸ *Blue spruce at rear (planted by previous owners) will grow too big for this courtyard, cloak the area with unwanted shade and suck moisture and nutrients from the soil. The bigger it becomes, the more costly it will be to remove.*

SUNDIALS *DO* WORK!

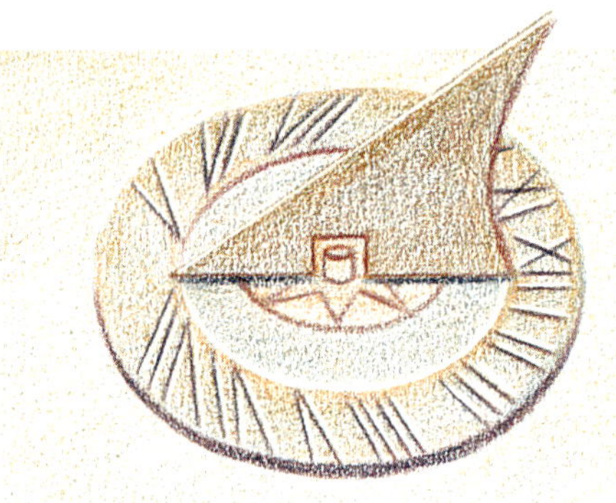

You just need one made for your hemisphere (north or south) and your latitude. In the northern hemisphere, the gnomon (the upright triangle) must point towards true north, while in the southern hemisphere you direct it to true south. The angle of the top edge of the gnomon relative to the dial face must equal the latitude of your garden. Sundials with adjustable gnomons can be set for any location.

1 *Paths can be given importance by their width and surface. The path on page 45 (A), relatively wide and solidly paved, is a major route; it leads from one public area (the front gate) to another (the main courtyard). In contrast, the stepping stones of this path indicate a way to a more private, less used part of the garden.*

2 *Statues and ornaments add interest and charm and help personalise your garden. One or two pieces look good, too many are distracting and messy. Sundials are most appropriate in open, sunny spots where they actually work.*

3 *An internal fence may seem pointless but the space it creates glimpsed through the gate is irresistible. People want to see what's in there and in this garden there is something to see, a tiny, sheltered courtyard devoted to shade loving plants.*

4 *This second courtyard could be used as a view garden for, say, a bathroom or bedroom; it could be a potting and storage area or, if sunny, a herb and vegetable patch.*

. . . there are still more secrets to discover. From the main courtyard a little path leads to a smaller enclosure created by an internal fence. This second courtyard is more private and can be closed off with a gate. From this, the second arm of the U, not shown, runs down the back of the house. This is a narrow, shady walkway, home for a collection of small ferns and other compact shade lovers.

Some plants used and their problems:

❶ *Banana relative develops very wide-spreading habit. Will become too big here.*

❷ *Cordyline has palm-like habit. Will eventually be just bare trunks at eye level but crown will cast shade.*

❸ *Spiny crown of this Livistona palm will spread into paved area.*

❹ *Citrus will be shaded out by surrounding trees. As it weakens it will become spindly and a target for insect attack.*

❺ *European silver birch will grow poorly in sub-tropical climate and cast increasing shade.*

❻ *Sapium sebiferum, a medium-sized tree, can reach 12m (40ft); too imposing here.*

❼ *Palm (Archontophoenix), with its canopy high overhead and a bare trunk at eye-level, will contribute only shade.*

❽ *Roses do not suit the sub-tropical look and will suffer as shade increases.*

A GARDEN IN REVIEW

What's Right and Wrong with this Solution?

Wanting a private, lush garden which they could use for outdoor eating, the owners of this small courtyard settled on a simple, geometric layout – linear, raised beds around the perimeter.

Raising garden beds creates a sense of enclosure by bringing plants closer to eye-level. It also gives the garden a structured look. More practically, it improves soil drainage and allows plants to be grown in better quality soil than the site might naturally have.

On the downside, the planting lacks unity and does not create an overall style or look. It's a 'one of everything' garden where the species chosen do not blend well with each other.

THE GARDEN IN BRIEF

- *The garden has a formal, geometric structure; linear, perimeter beds surrounding a rectangular shape. The rectangular table, centrally placed and pair of urns emphasise this symmetry.*
- *Planting is mixed and informal, yet size and layout of beds dictates an in-line placement. The result looks neither natural nor structured.*

Big Secrets

TURNING OPEN SPACES INTO PRIVATE, SECRET PLACES

This pretty, colourful garden is immaculately maintained for passers-by, however, it's too open to live in and there's little to draw you in; you can see everything from here.

Further from the city centre, gardens become bigger and they're not usually enclosed by high walls. On the contrary, they're often open to the street and dominated by grass. Perhaps there'll be a bed of flowers, a border of shrubs and a tree or two.

However, there's something you'll rarely find there – people; gardens that are open to view are rarely used. Owners enter these gardens only to maintain them, preferring to entertain or relax out of sight. What a waste!

Considering what it is worth, all the land that surrounds a home should form part of your daily living space and, with the enclosure and privacy that trees and shrubs buy, even your front yard will become a lovely and leafy outdoor 'room'.

This section presents ideas for creating an enclosure or enhancing an outlook in a more open garden. And we'll unearth some interesting entrances and pathways, and some delightful features and destinations found in gardens.

Designer: Michael Wayman

Made private with a perimeter planting of trees and shrubs, this garden is in constant use. As well as the summer house, there's a pool and a planting that invites exploration.

In a thickly planted garden, glimpses of little clearings through foliage heighten curiosity and anticipation of what else there is to see. Here a shrub has been used to enhance an outdoor 'room'.

Without these fence line shrubs, instead of a leafy outlook there'd be a panorama of passing traffic and the garden would be a virtual public park. This screen is too thin to be totally effective, especially from the footpath beyond, but it gives the garden a sense of enclosure, some shelter and quite a lot of privacy from the houses opposite. Notice how smaller shrubs have been used to fill in the gaps between taller, bare-trunked neighbours.

Fence Line Privacy

Shrubs Provide a Perfect Screen

For the homeowner craving privacy and bushier, more interesting surroundings, shrubs are the means to this end. There are thousands of them but those growing between 2 and 5 metres tall (6 and 16ft) are the best for creating fence line privacy.

For an informal screen of mixed shrubs, allow a depth of 3-4m (10-13ft) and plant at least two rows of shrubs, staggered rather than one behind the other. The more dense the planting, the more effective the screen. It will also make a better windbreak and small birds will be drawn to the food, shelter and nesting sites that a thick shrubbery provides. In return, they'll help to control grubs and insects that attack gardens during spring and summer.

When planting several rows of shrubs, remember the taller shrubs will cast shade on smaller ones.

So Tall and No Taller

How to determine the height of your screen

The height of the screen depends on the parts of the house or garden you want made private. If you want the whole house and garden to be invisible from the outside, go to the highest point, which may be a window inside the house, and determine what you don't want to see. Now determine how tall plants along your fence line need to be to block that line of sight. Keep the position of the sunny side in mind and remember the plants will cast shadows. The taller the plants, the longer the shadows cast. Should these shadows fall only on your neighbour's property, it's best to use plants that are only as tall as necessary. If a dense, 3m (10ft) shrub blocks the sight of a neighbour's house, why use something taller that will only hide the sky and cast longer shadows?

Before and after: Determine what you don't want to see from eye level then estimate the height screening plants need to be.

Designer: Garden Advisory Service

Right: In frost-free areas where height is required but ground space is restricted, palms are a good choice. These palms partially screen the neighbouring two storey house but the crowns are high enough to permit good views. A complete screen could be achieved by underplanting these tall palms (Archontophoenix cunninghamiana) *with smaller ones such as* Howea forsteriana, *creating two tiers of foliage.*

Tall, Narrow Choices for Cooler Climates

The trees listed here thrive in climates where winters are long and frosty. They are not recommended for frost-free gardens. Heights given are approximate usual maximums but, as your soil and climate can affect ultimate height, it's best to check locally before choosing.

- Chinese juniper *(Juniperus chinensis)* 20m (65ft)
- Dawyck beech *(Fagus sylvatica* 'Dawyck') 13m (43ft)
- Italian cypress *(Cupressus sempervirens)* 20m (65ft)
- Lombardy polar *(Populus nigra* 'Italica') 30m (100ft)
- Pencil cedar *(Juniperus virginiana)* 15m (50ft)
- *Prunus* 'Amanogawa' 9m (30ft)

Lorna Rose

Left: This gardener has created a very wide path between trees, shrubs and expanded garden beds that are brimming with flowers including Silenes and Irises. This successfully breaks up a big, rectangular lawn to form an interesting and private garden.

1. *Leptospermum petersonii*
2. *Kunzea ambigua*
3. *Myoporum floribundum*
4. *Banksia robur*
5. *Melaleuca incana*
6. *Eucalyptus erythrocorys*
7. *Banksia integrifolia*
8. *Acacia spectabilis*
9. *Senna artemisioides*

Above: The best individual shrubs for screens are thickly foliaged to the ground but in a deep, mixed planting, more open shrubs may be used together to produce an impenetrable mass. This screen of Australian shrubs combines dense and open shrubs for a good mix of foliage colours and textures. Now about 1.8m (6ft) tall, it will soon mature to a height of around 3m (10ft), blocking views into the property from the street. The success of the screen does not depend on these particular plants; a combination of your favourite shrubs could work just as well.

Lorna Rose

Trees as Screens

Trees are generally too tall for horizontal line of sight screening but they have a role to play where you are overlooked by a tall building. Umbrella-shaped trees, broad rather than tall with relatively low branches, give good ground level privacy without blocking light and views from the upper floors of a neighbouring building. Such trees add to your garden's intimacy and enclosure by providing a ceiling. Suitable species include frangipani, Japanese maple (Acer palmatum), *and various peach, almond and cherry varieties.*

To ensure privacy inside the house, a solid screen can be created anywhere between the windows and your fence line. We have suggested that the fence line is the most appropriate position as it will make your property private and probably won't block light from the house. A screen directly in front of the windows, such as this one, will block light and make cleaning the glass and painting the frames difficult. It contributes nothing to the garden's privacy.

Framing Views

Plants can enhance the picture

Right: On a hillside, this garden enjoys a spectacular panorama with no need for privacy from this direction. The screen, a clipped hedge of Xylosma congestum*, is kept low, more a safety fence than anything although it does block the sight of the roof of the house below. This plant makes a wonderfully compact screen and grows quickly in mild climates. It can be clipped or allowed to grow into a 5m (16ft) pendulous shrub. Summer flowers are fragrant but not showy. Tolerates -12°C (10°F).*

Designer: Garden Advisory Service

Left: Without the screen the outlook would be extensive, but the garden would be exposed to strong sea winds and direct views from the close neighbour at left. A good compromise was to cut a window into the screen to take in the view while losing no privacy and little shelter. The window is a stopover in the walk through the garden.

Rodney Hyett

This gardener has chosen a fast-growing passionfruit vine which will soon grow to cover this screen. A profusion of forget-me-nots, borage and cinerarias, and a flowering fruit tree completes the scene.

No Space for Plants?

Raise the fence

If you have a spot where it's not possible to plant a privacy screen, consider this relatively cheap structural alternative; you can raise the height of the dividing fence with panels of lattice and cover the lot with a vine.

ESTABLISHING A HEDGE

Unless your soil is rich and friable, you'll get best results by planting in a trench rather than individual holes. By digging a trench, a greater volume of soil is dug, aerated and improved, resulting in faster, more even growth. For a single row hedge, make the trench 60cm (2ft) wide and 30cm (1ft) deep. Double the width for a double row; double rows are deeper and more impenetrable.

Buy small, similarly sized plants, know their ultimate spread and space them accordingly, allowing for some intermingling of branches.

Start shaping straight away by trimming the young hedge to its formal shape. If you let the plants grow to the desired height first, you will never shape them properly nor will they be evenly dense. Shape so that the top is narrower than the base, or sunlight will not reach the lowest branches and they will die. Lightly shear whenever new growth exceeds 15cm (6in) but, where winters are always frosty, don't shear after late summer.

Designer: Raymond Hansen

Above: In mild climates, hedges of closely spaced Ficus benjamina *are favoured. They form a dense, evergreen screen fast but as the plants can grow into enormous trees, their use in hedges may not be wise long term. In sub-tropical climates, plant with caution and clip hard to restrict size.*

Right: In temperate to cold areas, Photinia hedges are popular with a profusion of evergreen leaves which are a startling red when young.

Clipped Hedges

THE TRADITIONAL MEANS TO ENCLOSURE AND PRIVACY

Clipped hedges make impenetrably dense screens and grand dividers, but to reach their potential they require a commitment of time and effort. Formal hedges usually need clipping two or three times a year.

The choice of plants should suit your area, soil and site; the last thing you want is death or dieback of one or more plants due to inappropriate climatic or soil conditions. This is a problem often encountered with hedges of conifers in mild to warm regions.

Small trees add height to a shrubbery but remain in scale and their foliage canopies create a perfect environment for shade-loving shrubs. Here, the squat, umbrella shaped flowering cherry, 'Mt Fuji', performs a spectacular double act with Rhododendron 'Suzette'.

Shrubs for Screens

How to Choose and Where to Use Them

All shrubs play a role in the creation of privacy screens but because their ultimate shapes, sizes and densities vary according to species, your job is to select those that will suit your site.

Allow plenty of depth

As well as the height desired, consider the lateral space. The more narrow this is, the harder it will be to grow an effective screen as your choice will be restricted to shrubs with narrow, upright habits (pencil pines, bamboos, clustering palms, Mahonia). Shrubs grow to be about as wide as they are tall and, although you can get away with less, a planting depth of 3m (10ft) will support a thick shrubbery of a similar height and deliver privacy.

Dense is best

Densely foliaged shrubs make the most effective screens and where planting depth is limited, it's best to stick to those shrubs. However, if you have 3 or 4m (10-13ft) of depth, the density of each species is not as important as you can grow three, four, even five rows of shrubs in that space.

Imagine the future

Start the screen by choosing the main components, that is, the biggest shrubs. Don't buy them until you have a clear vision of the fully grown plants where you propose to grow them. Unless you are familiar with the plants, try to find some mature specimens. Note their shapes, heights and spreads and any surroundings which may be influencing their habits.

Give them living space

When you are satisfied the desired shrubs will fit and do the job, buy and position them. Use smaller shrubs to fill out the screen but don't try to create instant privacy by over-planting. The shrubs will grow and must be given ground and air space for their roots and branches to spread. Too many shrubs in a space means too much competition for light, space, water and nutrients; the strongest will survive but they may be weakened in the process and forced to adopt unnatural and unappealing shapes.

Plan for shade

When planting a screen several rows deep, be aware of the shade that will be cast by the tallest and most dense shrubs. Avoid siting those needing full sun in a spot that will become shady. Instead, use expendable varieties that can be replaced with shade lovers. Shrubberies that lie in an east-west direction will be sunny mostly on one side; those that run north-south receive sun on both sides.

Spines for Security

To keep animals or intruders from your garden, consider shrubs with thorny branches or prickly foliage. However, you do have legal obligations; never place them where they could injure a passer-by or a person with legitimate business on your property and don't let them overhang neighbouring gardens.

What Shrubs Do

Some Examples of Shapes and Sizes

Growing a screen is a bit like building a wall except the components aren't full size when put together. However, the ultimate shapes and sizes of shrubs are fairly predictable and if you think in terms of what will be, rather than what is now, you'll improve your chances of creating a successful garden.

The shrubs shown here are different shapes and sizes and could be used to form part of a privacy screen. Some are big enough to screen on their own, others may be used to fill in gaps, for foliage colour or texture or to provide extra interest and variety. They are not the only shrubs you can use; they are presented as examples of the forms shrubs take and how you might use them, or others like them, to create enclosure and privacy.

When banking shrubs together, remember it's the foliage, not the flowers, that creates the effect for most of the year. The shape, size, colour and texture of leaves vary from shrub to shrub. Consider these characteristics and you can create a planting that's subtly beautiful for most or all of the year. If the shrubs you choose do flower at the same time, you'll want these colours to be complementary and to blend in with the rest of the garden.

***Red flowering currant* (Ribes sanguineum)**
A big, rounded, deciduous shrub that will give total privacy during the warmer months. It grows to about 3m (10ft) tall and as wide, accepts winter lows of -20°C (-4°F) and grows best in moist climates where winters are always long and frosty. Group a few together for an easy, informal hedge or use as a major shrub in a mixed screen. Flowers appear mid-spring to late spring.

***Golden candles* (Pachystachys lutea)**
Over-planting can produce good results; there are about 20 here. This tropical, soft-wooded shrub doesn't spread but grows upright to nearly 2m (6ft), forming a mass like a big, single shrub. Grow it in part or full shade. It needs a moist, humid frost-free climate. Flowers most of the year.

Cantua pyrifolia

Open and too lax on its own, grow the showy Cantua in a mixed bank of shrubs where branches of others offer it support and the density that's lacking. From tropical highlands, the shrub thrives where summers are mild and humid, winters cool and moist. It tolerates light frosts only, grows to 4m (13ft) and flowers appear in spring and sporadically through summer.

***California lilac* (Ceanothus sp)**

Hardy to about -10°C (14°F), Ceanothus form mounds of dense, evergreen leaves topped with vivid blue flowers in mid-spring. When crowded, shrubs may be relatively erect to nearly 3m (10ft) or more horizontally inclined if able to spread. Best in cool to mild climates with rain mostly in winter. It's possible to prune Ceanothus into the shape of a small tree.

***Mudgee wattle* (Acacia spectabilis)**

Complete solidity is not essential for an effective screen. Relatively open shrubs work well if there is depth, as the eye focuses on the mass of foliage, not on what can be seen through it. This wattle grows to nearly 4m (13ft) and has lovely ferny leaves and blue green bark similar to a silver birch. Brilliant yellow flowers appear in early spring. Takes -5°C (23°F).

***Silver Cassia* (Senna artemisioides)**

Use low-growing, bushy shrubs in front of taller, bare trunked species to create the impression of a solid wall of foliage. Sun lovers like this Senna wouldn't work on the shady side of a shrubbery but there are plenty of others that would. The silver Cassia is extremely drought resistant and tolerates a few degrees of frost. It grows to 1m (3ft) and flowers appear in winter.

Shrub Combinations That Work

Some pointers to success

- *Don't mix plants that have widely different needs or some will suffer from the needs of others. For example, natives of wet summer climates make poor partners for Mediterranean plants as the latter expect a dry summer.*

- *All shrubs can be pruned and, in doing so, will grow faster and become more dense.*

- *Know when to expect flowers and their colours to create pleasing colour combinations and have either a succession of blooms throughout the year or one or two massed seasonal displays.*

- *Like most plants, shrubs are out of flower most of the year so consider other attributes such as the colour and texture of the leaves, possibile autumn foliage and colourful and/or bird-attracting berries. Even the bark of some shrubs is attractive and worth considering.*

Banking Shrubs Together

The Art of Building a Garden

No matter how lovely a shrub, plant it in isolation and that's all it is – beautiful – and probably only while it's in flower. Plant it with other shrubs and it becomes useful as well, part of a shrubbery that delivers privacy and shelter, attracts birds and adds to the charm of your garden. Its beauty is magnified now there are combinations of colours and pleasing foliage contrasts. Instead of homing in on a single shrub, you appreciate the beauty and utility of the whole bank.

A deep, wedge-shaped planting makes the most effective screen.

Left: Just over 2m (6ft) deep, density is the feature of this fence line screen and the foliage plays a key decorative role. Yellow-spotted Aucuba and a golden conifer bring colour and contrast to the surrounding dark green foliage and the wavy, grey-green leaves of Pittosporum add movement and interest. Colour on this largely shady side is provided by a mix of perennial flowers, including Agapanthus, Crocosmia, lilies and Lychnus.

Right: Planted in tiers from ground covers through small, medium and big shrubs to trees behind, this wedge-shaped bank maximises display space and gives each plant plenty of sunlight. The trees at the rear, the neighbour's, have been successfully borrowed to give depth to this planting.

SPECIAL EFFECTS

A conifer collector makes a show of it

Lorna Rose

Gardeners sometimes become enthusiasts for one type of plant and devote their garden to their chosen love. For this gardener, it's ornamental conifers, a group of many species that come in a range of subtle foliage colours. All can be clipped into an endless variety of shapes and, for the unconventional gardener with a sculpting bent, this is their attraction. Years and a few pairs of shears later, the result is a private, sheltered garden unlike others.

Right: Attention to colour, texture and climatic combination means this grouping both looks good and grows well together. The leaves of the wattle (top) and Senna (bottom) are fine and ferny in appearance and grey-green in colour. In colour and texture they contrast well with the big, bold, olive-green leaves of the Banksia. From different parts of Australia, these plants all like full sun and about the same amount of water. Plants are (from top) Acacia spectabilis, Banksia robur *and* Senna artemisioides.

Solutions for Narrow Spaces

Screening is possible in spaces less than 1m (3ft) deep but your choice of plants is restricted. Look for narrow, upright growers such as pencil pines, bamboo, sacred bamboo or the two below.

Left: Producing many erect shoots from the base, Mahonia lomariifolia *forms a bamboo-like clump which can grow up to 4m (13ft) tall. The spiny leaves are clustered at the tops of stems, causing them to arch outwards. Yellow, nondescript flowers appear in winter followed by bluish berries. Spiny leaves make this a hazardous choice if there's a path nearby but it's a dramatic plant worth finding a spot for. Accepts winter lows of -15°C (2°F). Prefers afternoon shade.*

Right: In humid, frost-free gardens the many species of clustering Chamaedorea palms make elegant screens, even in narrow beds. They'll reach 4m (13ft) easily. The congested clumps arch outwards, however the canes can be held upright if passage is necessary. Plants will grow in full or part-shade, even sun if water is plentiful (though they will bleach there). There are several other species of slender, clustering palms, the Rhapis species being well known as an indoor plant. Outside it demands full shade.

Bamboo's Bad Habits

Although bamboo makes a beautiful and impenetrable screen fast, it has a major drawback; it spreads quickly and widely by underground runners and will soon overrun big areas of your, and your neighbour's, garden. One way to tame it is to grow it in large tubs. There are some clumping, non-running types. The sacred bamboo (*Nandina domestica*) is not a true bamboo and does not share the running habit.

ABOUT THE TRUMPET CREEPER

Campsis grows in cold and warm temperate climates. Prune hard in late winter, back to a main framework. Tolerates light shade in hot areas, elsewhere grows in full sun. Hardy to -20°C (4°F).

Above: Here's a good illustration of the benefits and costs of climbers. America's trumpet creeper (Campsis radicans)*, is showy, long blooming and a rampant grower. Used here, the dividing fence has been beautified and the mass of foliage has raised its height, adding to its usefulness as a screen.*

Right: Climbers don't have to be restricted to walls or boundary fences. To create a separate space or room within your garden, or screen a service area from view, consider climbers on free-standing trellises. This will use less lateral space than a bank of shrubs and take less time to grow. If space is no problem, climbers make a good background for shrubs, the combination often creating a wild, uncultivated look as here where the glossy evergreen leaves of the passionfruit, a native of Brazil, produce a quick, thick screen.

CLIMBERS

Exuberant growth means quick screening

As discussed earlier, climbers are heaven sent for the secret gardener. They can provide quick screening and produce masses of showy, exotic flowers. Best of all, their exuberant growth brings abundance to the garden design, a hint of the tangle of wilderness in the city, but watch how they grow. Like all climbers, the trumpet creeper, at left, has raced to the top of the fence where it forms a billowing mass of foliage.

The spirited growth will continue and, being unsupported, will fall over both sides of the fence, covering and smothering shrubs below or climbing into nearby trees. Pruning is necessary at least once a year if you choose to use vigorous climbers.

Lorna Rose

ABOUT THE PASSIONFRUIT VINE

The passionfruit or purple granadilla (Passiflora edulis) *is popular in frost-free and warmer gardens. A vigorous grower, prune early in spring. Needs rich soil, full sun, plenty of summer water.*

Inner Secrets

The Gardens Within the Walls, Behind the Hedges

Although enclosed and made private by a dense bank of fenceline shrubbery, this garden is as open as a playing field. From this vantage point at the back of the house, we take in the whole scene in a few seconds without focusing on anything. Without a path there's nothing to lead us into the garden, no suggestion that there might be something worth seeing here. Only the kids would use this garden and then, how long before they tire of their play equipment and seek the excitement and interest of the dense, bushy planting beyond?

What's the more interesting landscape, a prairie or a forest? One is open to the horizon in all directions, a vast sea of grass perhaps dotted here and there with a shrub or a lonely tree. Whatever's there can be seen from where you are. The other is enclosed, dense and full of life. There's a lot to see but it has to be sought out, explored.

Clearly, it's the forest where we'd rather spend a day because there's more to see and do there; it's a fun, mysterious and memorable place to visit.

It's the same with gardens; most are dominated by big areas of lawn but where's the interest, the mystery, the intrigue in that? A single glance sums it up, so why go there?

Secret gardens, however, are dense and bushy. They have secluded sun-traps and sheltered clearings; some contain small lawns ideal for basking in the sun but these spaces don't dominate the garden, rather they are delightful destinations to be discovered along the paths and winding tracks of the garden.

Lorna Rose

About the same size as the garden pictured at left, but that's where the similarity ends. This is a wild, woodsy garden, the extent and contents of which cannot be determined without further investigation. Your interest may settle on the distant summerhouse and you are instantly curious about this mysterious garden. Even if you've been here a hundred times before, you will still follow the path. A thickly planted, bushy garden remains a magnetic, interesting and satisfying place long after the initial curiosity about its contents and layout has been satisfied.

Right: Even if you live in the inner city, a secret garden can transport you to more natural surroundings. This Sydneysider only has to walk out his back door and he's in a gardener's impression of native bushland. Having a bush garden doesn't always mean it will be a shady garden. By keeping fence line plantings below the lowest position of noon sun in winter and filling the space in front with low shrubs, the bench remains sunny during the cooler months of the year.

GARDENS FOR KIDS

It's often said that expansive lawns are essential playgrounds for kids, but that's not always the case.

As they grow older and become more adventurous, they'll want to get out of their confined lawn space, teaming with other young grassland refugees to play interesting games in the nearest patch of bush! You'll find, too, they start to hanker for a hard surface for their bikes and scooters; the lawn just doesn't fit the bill here.

If you want to encourage them to play at home, forget the huge lawn and give them a densely planted, safe and shady garden, an adventure playground full of interesting hidey-holes, cubby house sites, winding tracks and trees to climb, and maybe, if you can't do without it, just a tiny patch of lawn.

Right: Keep it simple, keep it easy. A good way to achieve an attractive garden that needs minimum maintenance is to plant a lot of the same species. Choose a variety that suits your climate and conditions. Here, a mass of tree ferns has turned a tiny, sloping city garden into a rainforest. Maintenance is limited to an annual mulching of the soil (to simulate natural leaf litter) and watering during dry spells.

Lorna Rose

Above: Views are important in thickly planted secret gardens as they create an impression of space and distance that counterbalance the mass of foliage. They also lead the eye through the garden to interesting places along the paths. Most gardens don't have impressive natural outlooks but internal views can be created. Here, use has been made of a neighbouring church; glimpses of the old facade provide a backdrop to entice visitors into the garden for a closer look.

Below: Some open, sunny areas are desirable in all gardens but lawn is not the only means of achieving this. Broad plantings of annual and perennial flowers, such as lavender, Sisyrinchiums and Achillea and low shrubs, create this colourful, open and sunny space that's more interesting than a monoculture of grass. True, you can't walk on it, but you can cut a path through it and have the added benefits of the colour and fragrance of flowers and the movement of birds and butterflies that are drawn to them.

Leigh Clapp

Above: A secret garden can be as sunny, like this one, or shady as you like. If you want to maximise the amount of sun you receive, minimise the use of big, spreading trees. Instead, use dense shrubs 3-4m (10-13ft) tall for enclosure, privacy and wind shelter. This is one of several sections of a garden, each separated by walls of taller shrubs. The result is a collection of open spaces, each carpeted with ground-covering shrubs and sun-loving flowers, such as the lilies and Alliums shown.

Gardens within Gardens

Creating Private Rooms in Larger Gardens

The bigger your garden, the more opportunities to indulge your landscaping fantasies. With increasing space comes the chance to experiment. You could have a number of styles in the one garden; perhaps enclosure, privacy and density in one section and more traditional open lawns and borders elsewhere. Maybe you want a hidden, secret spot where you can relax or entertain surrounded by nature.

By creating an enclosed space within a garden, you draw attention to the enclosure. Why is this area enclosed, people ask. Privacy and shelter is the practical answer but, having created it, ensure that you will want to use it by making the planting especially appealing or different.

In the following pages you'll find some interesting ways to create gardens within gardens.

Walled off from the rest of the garden by banks of shrubs and planted in a different style, this is a distinct space within a larger garden. It's a highlight of a stroll through the garden, an unexpected clearing, sheltered and sunny and rich with the colour and fragrance of massed roses bordered with aromatic catmint.

Lorna Rose

Design Tip

We recommend that paths be built at least 1.5m (5ft), preferably 1.8m (6ft) wide. You will be tempted to narrow them but plants grown either side will spill onto the path, narrowing and softening the edges. This will hamper an already narrow path such as this one where the catmint hinders clear passage.

Right: This little suntrap, separated from the garden by a lattice fence, has a striking difference; every plant has white flowers. Plantings in shades of the one colour have appeal; they're subtle and elegant and, if you are uncertain of your taste in colour combinations, they're an easy solution. Note the covered seating alcove built into the wall at rear. Flower gardens are necessarily open, sunny places but, for safe and comfortable extended visits, people need shade. The bench faces the sunny side which makes it usable year round. In winter, sunlight streams into the alcove from a low angle but, as the sun climbs higher and the days get hotter, the roofed alcove becomes more shady.

Lorna Rose

Above: If you can't choose between the various styles of garden you'd like, don't try. Instead, divide the garden into different spaces and design each as a separate entity. Here, the gardener was torn between the impressive formality of clipped hedges, topiary and neat lawns and a love of variety and the natural exuberance of massed shrubs. The contrast couldn't be more striking but that's its appeal.

An Enclosure In The Making

Only a couple of years old, this bay will become increasingly sheltered and shady as its plantings grow. The bank of maples and Rhododendrons will rise to hide the fence and eventually the roof behind, while the flowering cherry trees at the front will join together to form an arched entrance.

As growth continues, expect to remove some shrubs to give others room to spread. The border of sun-loving annuals will also need to be changed to suit the increased shade.

Three Ways to Create an Enclosure

A frame around your secret garden

1. The 'Natural'

Just as shrubs, informally grouped together, can screen your boundaries, they may be used within the garden to create different spaces. Here, a grassy path leads from one space to another through an arch which frames a Rhododendron in full bloom. A glimpse of something interesting in the next space draws you in. Here a spectacular shrub has been used but its effect is seasonal. Other possibilities include statues, ornaments, sculptures, structures or views.

2. The Structural

Left: The quickest way to create a division is to build a fence but it will be a prominent feature so choose a style and materials that will suit your garden. This fence of saplings is suitably rustic for the rambling country garden; it would not suit more formal surroundings.

3. The Formal

Right: Clipped hedges can be used to create internal divisions. They are less space-consuming than an informal shrubbery, demand more maintenance and, although the hedges themselves are stiff and formal, the plantings they contain need not be. Walk between one space and another via a simple gap in the hedge or build a more elaborate structure such as this arched arbour.

Left: This decorative arch displays its climbing rose beautifully but from a garden design point of view there's no reason for it; it signals no change and frames no view or feature and exists only to support the rose.

Below: The arch doesn't have to be big and, if the change it signifies isn't great, a simple, almost invisible structure may be best. Here, a very plain wire arch, softened and obscured by plants, draws little attention to itself while marking the boundary between the front garden and narrow side passage.

Arches and Arbours

How to Use them Effectively

Built features can be useful and decorative. An arch, for instance, has pulling power; there's a suggestion of it leading to something. If it's obvious what's ahead and it's not much different from where you are, this pull will be lost; its only purpose would be to hold up a climber.

In the garden on page 79, for example, the arch suggests a change. It's a door in a wall which stops you from seeing what's beyond; you must go through it to find out and, once through, there *is* change. Gone is the openness of the rose garden, replaced by banks of shrubs and flower beds.

*Above: Two sheds divide this garden into ornamental plantings on this side and a service area on the other. The passage between the two has been highlighted by an arch covered with golden hops (*Humulus lupulus* 'Aureus').*

Below: You know it's just a swimming pool but a glimpse of its waters through a door in a hedge is enough to draw you in for a look. Take the hedge away and you'd see it all from here.

Inviting Entrances

Memorable Gardens Start at the Front Gate

The secret garden of this city townhouse is behind the screen of orange-flowered Streptosolen jamesonii ***and pink climbing geraniums. To get to it, you pass through this small, sunny streetside planting, an astonishing mix of spring flowers, including Babiana, Freesias, Ranunculus, forget-me-nots and heartsease. Massed flowers lift the spirits, especially when planted in such an unrestrained manner.***

If every time you come home you're pleased by what you see through the front gate, you've created a winner, a garden that makes you happy to be home. It will have that effect on others, too.

If you live in the suburbs, don't consider the strip of land outside your front fence as the responsiblity of the local council. They don't have the resources to care for it properly and you'll benefit most from any improvement so try taking on the task yourself. We've never heard of a council objecting to a resident beautifying public land, but it's best to enquire first in case there are regulations.

Plantings outside your front fence add depth and density to your own privacy screen, increase the impact and size of your garden and stir the interest of neighbours by improving your section of street. Others may follow and that can only improve the value of your precinct.

Tim Griffith

Losing planks but none of its charm, a weather- beaten lichgate makes a delightful entrance to a wild, country-style garden. Shrubs and the young wattle (Acacia baileyana) and pepper trees either side help to naturalise the structure.

Above: Although most of us don't have unpaved driveways we can still make them look like country lanes with the plants we choose to use beside them. A tunnel of foliage formed by over-arching branches is the main attraction here and it not only looks good, it's practical in that it keeps any cars below cool. Use trees if you have room (that's a silver birch on the left) or big, tree-like shrubs like the Cotoneaster at right.

Right: If your garden is enclosed by a high wall, you have little opportunity to make the entrance inviting from the outside but, because what's behind the wall is unseen, you can surprise guests when the gate is opened. As you approach this garden, you are met with a hedge of Ficus benjamina *and a steel door but, once inside, an unexpected landscape of dry climate plants is laid before you.*

Mystery and Surprise

One look and it's gone?

We've talked about the elements of mystery and surprise that secret gardens possess. We've said that by making them dense and bushy you'll create curiosity and a desire to explore. But once it's seen, surely all the mystery and surprise is gone, all curiosity satisfied?

Happily, no! As the layout of the garden becomes known, you'll still be lured down the disappearing path you've been down countless times. Along the way, you'll still be thrilled by a lovely vista that you have created; mystifed by what will be in flower today; surprised by the first daffodil or the sight of a family of finches nesting in the dense shrubbery.

Right: A young wattle tree (Acacia spectabilis) *and* Dracaena draco *behind the fence were sited either side of the path to form a tunnel of shade at the entrance. Set back and partially obscured by the outer planting, there's an air of mystery about this gate and the garden beyond.*

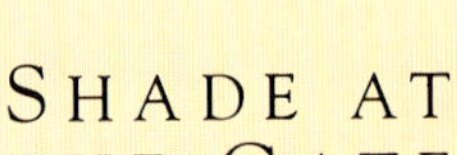

SHADE AT THE GATE

Imagine this; it's summer and you're walking home. You're tired and cranky and just want to get out of the heat and glare. When you get to your gate, you step under a spreading tree into deep, cool shade. What bliss! You instantly feel glad to be home.

Shade at the gate is physically and emotionally comforting. Like a house, trees signify shelter and safety and humans prefer the cover and protection of trees to the feeling of open spaces. Shade your gate and you will create a lasting, pleasing impression.

Above: Entrances that pass through tall hedges or thick shrubberies create an enticing, framed view of the garden. An arbour supporting a dense vine makes the entrance to this garden look so inviting. The picket gate and the flowering currant (Ribes sp) *add to the garden's country cottage-style appeal.*

There's no need to make little-used paths wide, but do consider the spread of plants before siting them either side. Put wide plants too close to the edges and you'll soon lose the path. Note how the lengthwise placement of the bricks gives the path a river-like flow.

Making Tracks

Paths Reveal the Garden's Secrets

Of all the secret garden features, two are essential; plants and a path.

Paths are what pull you into the garden. They are the means by which you explore, maintain and admire it and their layout is important to the success of your garden design.

Plan the route carefully

To establish where a path should go, walk around the site of your new garden. While you are considering where to put foliage, position the clearings and utility areas and other major features, think about how you are going to get around them. Then walk out your proposed paths. Are they convenient and practical? Will they make an attractive stroll when all the plants are fully grown?

Paths don't go just anywhere; they are designed to take you on a scenic walk via destinations such as seating and eating areas, water features, individual garden 'rooms' or lookouts with views.

Even in a tiny garden you can have a good, all-weather path and space for plants. Here, concrete slabs topped with slate tiles provide firm footing; big gaps between them permit a planting of baby's tears (Soleirolia). Use thyme or snow-in summer in colder climates.

Designer: Raymond Hansen (garden at right)

Garrie Maguire

Some layout ideas

You don't want paths everywhere or you'll lose planting space and won't achieve the density of a true secret garden. However, you need relatively easy access to every part of the garden so you can walk through it to view and maintain it.

A circuit (a loop, or crescent) is a good basic layout that gives you a long stroll and good access. Try to avoid dead-ends; these can be irritating and you'll find that you won't go down there, except to work. If a dead-end is unavoidable, create a reason for going there. This could be seating and a pond, fountain or statue, or your collection of rare and beautiful orchids.

Don't go straight

In informal gardens, straight paths look forced onto the landscape whereas curves have a natural flow, like a restful and romantic stream.

The route should sweep towards the destination, not wiggle its way there. Too many bends in too short a space look silly when there's no reason for them. If there's an obstruction such as a tree, bend the path around it but don't build a meander just to have one; it will only encourage short-cutting and you'll end up with too much path, not enough garden.

Don't skimp on width

The width of a path depends on its importance, how you use the garden and the space you have to play

Building a Path of Bricks or Pavers

For paths of brick or unit pavers, firm foundations will help prevent cracking and subsidence. Uneven paths look unsightly, collect water and can be uncomfortable and dangerous to walk on.

Firm foundations are the key when building a paved pathway that's even, comfortable and safe to walk on.

Simple Steps to Success

1. *Dig out the route of the path to the depth of the units plus 100mm (4in). Remove any tree roots.*
2. *Lay 75mm (3in) of crushed rock that contains a lot of fine material. Compact this.*
3. *Overlay with 25mm (1in) of sand. Level and compact.*
4. *Lay paving units. Tap into base and together with a rubber mallet.*
5. *Fill cracks between units with fine, dry sand brushed into them.*

with. Wide paths have grandeur, so make entrance ways and other major paths 1.8m (6ft) wide, enough space for two people to stroll along abreast. Try to keep paths this wide, especially if, like most gardeners, you like to show visitors around the garden, because walking abreast makes conversation easier than in single file.

Most gardeners won't have the room for such wide paths and settle for single tracks. If this is your problem, try to keep single paths at least 1m (3ft) wide. Only seldom-used paths should be allowed to degenerate into very narrow tracks.

A walk through the garden should be a pleasant stroll. You don't want to be kicking plants away from your feet or pushing past branches.

Surface suggestions

You can surface paths with many different materials. Hard paving such as concrete, stone or bricks are the most durable materials and they keep feet clean. On the downside, it can be costly, must be laid well or it will crack or slump, and can look too artificial in some settings.

Loose paving such as pea gravel, (rounded river stones about 10mm (⅓in) in diameter), or bark chips is cheap to buy, easy to lay and clean but can be uncomfortable to walk on, especially in bare feet, and is only suitable for level sites.

Grass is soft on the feet, easy on the eye and suited to well-watered, English-style gardens. However it's not very durable on high-traffic paths, may be soft and sodden after heavy rain and needs a lot of sun. Maintenance includes mowing, weeding, feeding, watering and trimming edges.

Rammed earth can suit the look of bushy gardens but muddy footsteps traipsed through the house won't endear it to the occupants. It's best in dry climate areas or in outer parts of big, rambling gardens.

Before you decide on a material, consider its effect on the look you want to achieve and the other building materials used in your house and garden. If bricks, stone or concrete are already evident, using more of the same would create a unified result and would better suit its environment than would the introduction of another vastly different element.

Paths of brick or stone look good, can last a lifetime and are firm underfoot whatever the weather. Here, both materials have been used in a path that oozes rustic charm and is well-suited to its informal, English cottage surroundings.

Other points to consider:

- *Periodic changes of surface (from brick to stone) relieve the monotony of bricks and, being laid across the run of bricks, make the path seem wider.*
- *Edging stones, longer than the bricks and deeply sunk, prevent the path from breaking up through sideways movement.*
- *Subsidence has caused the step to crack. Prevent this with good foundations.*
- *This pattern (stretcher bond) is the easiest to lay but there are fancier finishes.*
- *Bricks and stone are absorbent. In shady, moist areas they can become coated with slippery slime. Where winters are so cold the ground freezes, they will crack or flake with freezing and thawing.*

Left: ***This grassy path looks longer than it is thanks to an optical illusion. It is wider at this end than the other and the progressive narrowing gives the impression of distance. This can be a useful gimmick but it only works in one direction.***

Other points to consider:

- *Width lets two walk abreast.*
- *Just two shallow curves, forming an elongated S, give the path a natural flow.*
- *There's a reason for the curve; the path twists between two big shrubs.*
- *Clump of bright yellow Primulas captures your interest and draws you down the path. At other times of the year adjacent shrubs do a similar job.*
- *Path veers out of sight which creates an expectation that there's more to see.*

Lorna Rose

Right: ***In newly laid gardens, where plants are all seedlings or saplings, paths 1m (3ft) and more across look too wide. If you have a small garden you'll think you're wasting planting space and be tempted to narrow the paths but just remember, as plants grow upwards and outwards, the paths will begin to look more in scale. As growth continues, the plants will start to spread over the edges of the paths, narrowing them. This picture shows what can happen in just a few months. The path has been reduced to a very narrow track and may close over completely.***

Other points to consider:

- *Even if foot traffic keeps this track clear, plants will take root in the path area and the initial effort involved in laying it will be wasted.*
- *Without definite, clear paths, you lose the freedom to move about comfortably and the open space that's so necessary to balance the foliage masses.*
- *Earth surface looks lovely and natural but ensure it drains fast by using fine gravel and sand.*

Who could resist a stroll down this trail? Bordered with bluebells, azaleas, violets and forget-me-nots and roofed with a magnificent crab apple, there's interest everywhere and we still want to see what is round the next corner?

Other points to consider:

- *Gentle curves and earth surface give the path the look of a stream bed.*
- *Earth surface looks natural and suits a low-traffic garden; however it would not be walker- friendly after rain. Also, worn, compacted soil may become weedy in summer.*
- *Too shady for grass; hard paving or gravel are alternatives.*

Not a wilderness but a big garden where nature is valued more than neatness and control. Here, a narrow track hacked through the undergrowth makes a more appropriate passage than a wide or paved path. It's a secret trail both kids and adults would love.

Right: Here's a good example of how to use curves in garden design. This path sweeps away in a single, graceful curve. It has strength and movement, like a river current that propels you through the garden. A path that wiggled right and left over this distance would lack grace and look pointless.

Left: A tempting detour off the garden's main brick path (just visible at right) takes us through a rainforest gully before rejoining a few metres from here. This is a very small garden; you can see the fence, yet when you're in the gully it feels like a remote national park.

Other points to consider:

- *Surface of old railway sleepers and gravel is durable and clean.*
- *Surface is more informal than the main brick path and that suits the wild, natural style of the surrounding planting.*
- *Change of level adds visual interest while path that disappears into a tunnel-like void stirs curiosity.*

ROCKS IN A STRUCTURAL ROLE

Rocks don't have to look natural to be a strong garden feature. The square stones give this garden the look of a ruin, just as you would imagine a section of a lost city which will soon be reclaimed by the surrounding forest. Plants used here include Camellia, dwarf conifers, maples, and azaleas.

Sidelights

PERSONALISE YOUR GARDEN WITH ORNAMENTS

Ornaments can be striking objects that draw the eye, or subtle pieces that blend in with the garden and help to establish a mood or look without drawing attention to themselves. Whatever they are, they should be selected and sited with restraint; while two or three beautiful pieces can add richness, a garden full of lesser items is likely to suffer.

In the secret garden, ornaments that are natural (such as rocks, logs, even special plants) or unusual (such as artefacts, sculptures or home-made rustic furniture) are most successful and help stamp your personality on the garden.

Boulders, old stumps and logs are seen in wild places and, when you add them to a garden planted in a natural style, they make a wilderness style more believable. If they're beautifully individual, intricately marked or patterned, so much the better because their natural character and charm will further transform your garden.

Artificial objects have more impact. They are not meant to be subtle, rather they are there to be seen, touched and discussed. With an unusual ornament set in a space full of plants, you can show your style and attract people's attention.

HOW TO CHOOSE AND PLACE ROCKS

- *Choose only one type of stone. If you already have stone on your property or can see an outcrop from your garden, use that type.*
- *Not all rocks are equally attractive. White rocks can look featureless and are too reflective in summer. Cut stones look artificial and even naturally squared blocks have limited uses.*
- *Look for interesting shapes and signs of weathering or age, such as lichen, moss or discolouration.*
- *If buying several boulders for the one grouping, choose a variety of sizes.*
- *Odd numbers of rocks make the most pleasing groups and triangular arrangements are generally the most successful.*
- *Choose the site and plan their arrangement before the rocks arrive. Test various arrangements by using small items that have the same proportions as the rocks you have chosen, maybe using eggs, fruit, cans and cups. Move them about on a tabletop until you find a pleasing arrangement.*
- *Place the rocks with the most attractive face forward and bury each so that it grows upwards and inwards from ground level. You may have to bury up to half the stone but the finished result will look solid and believable.*
- *If the rocks have strata lines through them, lay the rocks with all the lines running in the same direction. Horizontal or inclined strata lines look convincing, vertical lines do not.*
- *For inspiration, study natural rock outcrops. When you see a grouping that appeals, no matter how big or small it is, consider what it is about its proportions or arrangement that you like.*

Rodney Hyett

ROCKS IN A SUBTLE ROLE

Smaller, easier to handle rocks have a more subtle role to play. They'll never be major features but can reinforce a natural look and their rough textures, earthy colours and solidity make a good contrast with the softness and lightness of surrounding plants. When engulfed by a sea of foliage, such as the Helianthus and Aquilegias shown here, rocks don't have to be set well into the soil because only their tops are revealed above the plants.

PICTURES WITH PLANTS AND PROPS

Small plants will make eye-catching pathside features but, to attract attention, they need to be dramatically different from the surrounding planting. These Sempervivums or houseleeks fit the bill and are given extra prominence by being raised on decorative concrete pedestals shared with a small ornament. A carpet of baby's tears (Soleirolia) completes the picture. Other strongly-shaped plants you could use include succulents such as Echeverias, Sedums and Crassulas, many of the small cacti and in mild winter areas, bromeliads and Tillandsias.

BRIDGES IN GARDENS

A sort of bridge fairies would build, this lovely log structure has a makeshift charm that's perfect for this dense, rainforest garden. Whenever you add an ornament or feature, keep in mind the garden's total look to ensure your addition will add to, not detract, from that.

DESIGN TIP

It's not easy building a convincing bridge in a garden. Firstly you must have something for it to cross and that 'something' must be convincing, not a little pond stuck in the middle of nowhere just to have a bridge over it. You wouldn't build a bridge over a little pond, you'd take the path around it and what's that little pond doing there, anyway? Better to build a bigger pond or create a stream.

If you have a place for a bridge, ensure that its style will suit your garden. You may love the red lacquered Japanese bridge you saw at the garden centre, but will it suit the style of garden you are creating?

FURNITURE AS A FEATURE

Tim Griffith

Apart from being functional, furniture has a decorative role to play so it needs to be something special. It may be an odd-looking, rare or very old piece of furniture. This chair has a weather-worn look, an unusual shape and makes a charming feature in a cottage garden.

PICTURESQUE RELICS

Just as you would find them in a natural forest, old, rotting logs or stumps are a likely accessory for woodsy gardens. Like rocks, they break up and contrast with expanses of foliage but they are much easier to lift and install. If you bring an old log home from the country it's a good idea to soak it in an insecticide solution in case it is harbouring termites.

Lorna Rose

GROWING ON TREES

In the wild, plants do grow on trees. Epiphytic orchids and bromeliads, and Tillandsias like these pictured above, anchor themselves to the high branches of forest trees, absorbing all their needs from rain and fortuitous animal droppings. In the garden, old, weatherbeaten logs not only make marvellous natural sculptures, they also give the gardener an extra niche for a new class of plants. Where winters are frosty, these plants will grow in a bright room.

LOOK AT THIS!

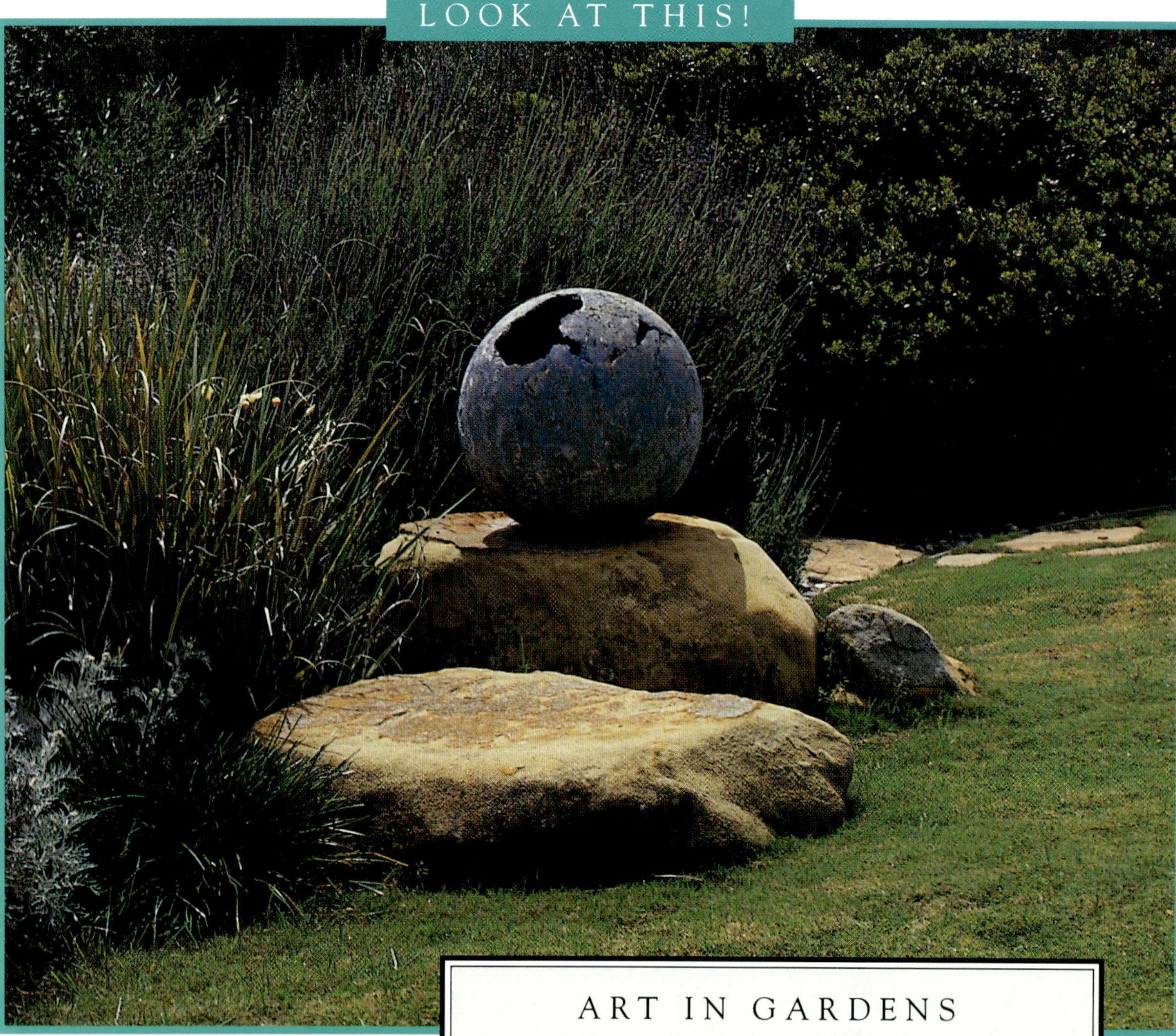

ART IN GARDENS

Art objects have been used to decorate gardens for centuries. In informal gardens, virtually anything that's weatherproof will suit. However, if you have a highly stylised or formal garden you will need to ensure that your choice blends in with the garden's look. For example, a classical, white marble bust would look out of place in a Japanese-style garden.

Above: Though it may be expensive, a big, original artwork can be the best use of your decoration budget. If it's imposing enough, you'll only need one object and its originality ensures that it will never go out of style. This ceramic ball on an impressive sandstone base is big enough to catch attention from anywhere in the garden. Here it is sited on the far side of a lawn to draw people across, then down into the more heavily planted parts of the garden. A smaller item or something common, something often seen in other gardens or shops, may not prove to be intriguing enough.

Right: Small ornaments won't attract attention from afar so can't be used as focal points. Instead, think of them as items of extra interest to be seen in passing, say, beside a path or at some destination within the garden. This strange bird is just one of many objects found in a garden that successfully breaks the restraint rule. It's full of welded sculptures, carved rocks and odd bits of machinery. The plants are equally curious – lots of stiff, strong shapes, sharp edges and spines. This is why it works; there's a unity, an alien quality about the place that's rivetting.

A PATHSIDE DISTRACTION

Water Features

Water, a Wonderful Addition to any Garden

Since gardens were first designed, water has been considered a desirable feature, cool and calming to the eye while the sound of the drips and splashes from fountains or falls is soothing and restful.

Choosing a site

The site for a water feature can be sunny or shady. At least some sun is desirable if you want to keep fish and the more sun the site gets the wider your choice of possible water plants. The most popular water plants, water lilies, demand full sun.

Be sure to consider the future effects of young trees and shrubs you want planted around the water feature. They will cast increasing shade as they grow which may make present plantings untenable.

If you have a sloping garden and are considering a natural-looking, mini-lake, remember the physics of water; it flows to and collects in low points, not on high ground, so siting it in the lowest part of the garden seems natural. This is not important for a formal structure or a fountain.

Fountains and waterfalls must be powered and, although low-voltage lines are easily run through the garden, they need to be connected through a transformer to an electric socket accessible from outside.

The bigger the pond, the better?

The surface area and depth of a pond has a big impact on the rate of evaporation and temperature of the water, which affects fish and plants. Generally, the bigger the pond the better, especially in the sun. Small sunny ponds evaporate fast and the temperature of the water fluctuates too widely for the good health of fish and plants. Small ponds in the shade are more stable but neither fish nor many water plants thrive in permanent shade.

If you haven't the space for a big pond, then make it deep, 45-60cm (18in-2ft) (the latter depth in the sun) as this will help stabilise water temperature and minimise evaporation. Avoid a big area of shallow water, under 45cm (18in).

What style to choose

Let the look of your garden influence you here. If you have a bush or forest style of secret garden, a natural looking pond or stream would suit whereas this would look out of place in the middle of a lawn. More structured, geometrically shaped ponds suit developed parts of the garden such as paved areas or lawns.

In a tiny courtyard, this fountain, arch and an optical illusion create an intriguing feature that seems to create more space than it consumes. The trick is the mirror attached to the courtyard wall, an apparent window into a garden beyond. The black-painted border which surrounds it, coupled with the wire arch that juts out from the wall, creates the illusion of depth.The fountain, a tiered model popular last century, suits the Victorian house and is a good, compact size for the small courtyard garden. Its cascading waters sound restful and help raise local humidity around the moisture-loving plants (including Hydrangeas, Camellias, Gardenias, Primulas, azaleas and a tree fern).

Enhancing an atrium of an inner-city terrace, this wall-mounted fountain containing duck weed has a pump built-in behind. To achieve this, a groove was chipped into the brickwork for the power line. Note the encroaching Virginia creeper which will soon grow to cover the wall.

Left: Surrounded by a big, brick paved terrace, a natural-style rockpool would have looked out of place here. The structured, formal environs call for this formal pool and wall fountain. Keep the big picture in mind, the look and feel of your whole garden, when planning individual elements. It's easy to focus on a component and lose sight of its effect on the whole.

Above: Water features can be simple decorative elements rather than major structures, especially in very small gardens. This Japanese water basin takes up little space yet contributes the soothing sound of falling water and the cool look of wet rock. Replace the bamboo pipe and ladle with, say, an old iron hand pump and suddenly eastern-style is transformed into western-style.

Fish, Plants & Ponds

Some points to remember

- *Fish keep the pond free of mosquitoes and help control excessive algae. They need at least a few hours' sun a day and water 45cm (18in) deep to help protect them from cats and birds, and provide a more stable water temperature.*
- *Provide additional shelter with caves of brick or stone or lengths of terracotta pipe on the bottom.*
- *Don't overstock. Too many fish in a given volume of water will deoxygenate it which in turn harms the fish and assists the growth of algae.*
- *Do not pollute the water with excessive fish food.*
- *The shadier the pond the fewer water plants you can grow. Waterlilies demand full sun.*
- *There are water plants for different depths. Waterlilies prefer depths of 45-60cm (18in-2ft).*
- *A single waterlily needs one square metre of water surface over which to spread. Other floating plants also need room to spread.*
- *The best looking ponds have a balance between open water and aquatic plants. Plants should cover no more than one-third of the water surface area.*
- *For healthy water and fish, grow nine, submerged, oxygenating plants per square metre of water surface in pots of soil on the bottom.*

Catch the sun, enjoy the view. At the end of a walk that winds through this small woodsy garden was a little space that caught a shaft of sun for a few hours in the mornings. It had a view over the pond and into the garden that made it a logical place for a bench. The path ends here so rather than a dead-end, the space has become a destination, a place at which you're happy to stay awhile. Note, how unobtrusive is the rough log bench; it melds with the garden, becoming almost invisible when unoccupied.

Secret Spots

Soak up the Sun or Shelter from it

Leigh Clapp

Open to the sun but sheltered from behind and on two sides, a little U-shaped clearing becomes a personal sun-trap for a few dreamy hours. You can almost feel the warmth from here; the afternoon light, reflected by the golden hops, made yellow and warm.

Sit in the sun or shelter from it, see but be unseen; the secret places are favourite garden spaces.

As your secret garden grows, a little place will develop that you'll become attached to. It will be sheltered and secluded, an intimate space to go to alone to read and relax.

You may not have planned your special spot; it may have developed by chance, a fortuitous niche among trees and shrubs planted for another purpose. You may find it by accident, too. Perhaps you'll be there on a maintenance task and notice its special ambience. It may be calm, sunny and warm on a day when there's a cold wind blowing or maybe it's a summer spot, cool and airy when the heat is oppressive. Equally, it may be the fragrance, the birds or the light that attracts you. Whatever it is, you'll soon find yourself using your secret spot when you need time alone in the garden.

Left: This area, about 3m (10ft) square, was designed as a flower lover's hideaway. It is surrounded by a fence largely hidden by flowers, and is entered through a vine-covered, romantic arch under which we're standing. The result is a sunny and colourful 'room', brightened with a mixture of daisies, Campanulas and other flowers.

Right: A sunny, sheltered, L-shaped corner of the house seemed the perfect place to display a collection of maples and a golden Robinia. But as they grew into small trees, another opportunity presented itself. The spreading canopies met, forming a shady cave with a lovely view of the garden. Now, with a bench and a little level paving, it's a place to take a cuppa and the Sunday papers.

Lorna Rose

Above: The centrepiece of this fragrant hideaway is a magnificent 'Cecile Brunner' rose, standardised into a small tree. Climbing roses spill over the surrounding hedges, too, which contain and concentrate the sweet fragrances. In season, this is a popular place for the gardener who comes to take in the beauty and perfume of favourite plants.

The Live-in Garden

Gardens Aren't Just for Looking At

A pergola is not the only option for structural shade. You could choose one of the many summer houses or gazebos on the market or have a pavilion built to your own design. This purpose-built tent shelters a table for six and may be demounted and stored during winter. Its whimsical, Camelot-influenced design would not suit a wild landscape but fits in well with this developed, formal layout.

Gardens aren't just for looking at, they're for living in, for eating, reading, sunning or snoozing. Include places for people and you'll multiply the pleasure and utility of your garden.

People places are spacious enough to accommodate groups but sheltered enough to maximise their use all year. They should be shady in summer, sunny when it's cool, paved rather than grassed, private and intimate and, for ease of catering, close to the kitchen. Remember, even the best garden furniture will go unused if in an unsheltered position.

Eating out at home

Take a perfect summer day and a group of your favourite people, set up a table in the garden with good food and wine and you have the makings of a long, enjoyable lunch.

The ability to eat and entertain comfortably in the garden is one of the great rewards for the effort of creating it. Once you've experienced the casual ambience of lunch in the garden, you can bet that outdoor meals will become a regular event.

Originally conceived as sheltered places from which to view the garden, gazebos today are more often a feature to be viewed. They are really only successful in larger gardens where they can be sited so as to be seen from afar; an intriguing destination glimpsed through the greenery. If possible, site where the view outwards is pleasant, too. Here the gazebo has both a watery and leafy outlook.

Part House, Part Garden

The convenience of a terrace

A terrace or deck off the house is the most convenient place to enjoy an outdoor lifestyle. The two spaces shown here have taken on the role of open-air living rooms with direct access to the house. Proximity to the kitchen makes for the easy provision of food and drink and should electricity be needed, there are always power points nearby.

Keep convenience of use in mind when designing outdoor living spaces. If the area is too far or too hard to reach, you'll be less inclined to use it; catering for gatherings there will involve too much to-ing and fro-ing from the kitchen.

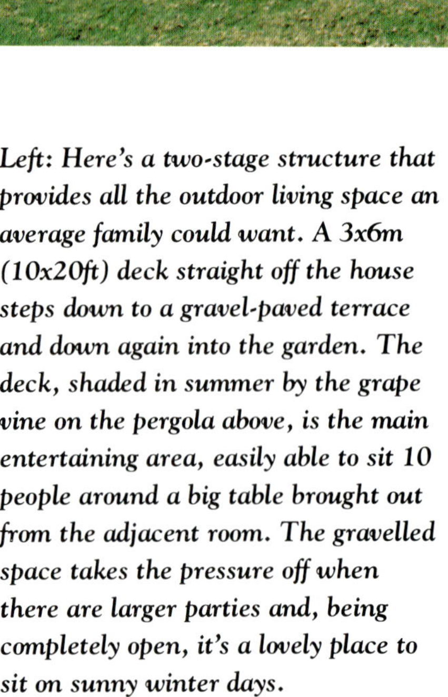

Left: Here's a two-stage structure that provides all the outdoor living space an average family could want. A 3x6m (10x20ft) deck straight off the house steps down to a gravel-paved terrace and down again into the garden. The deck, shaded in summer by the grape vine on the pergola above, is the main entertaining area, easily able to sit 10 people around a big table brought out from the adjacent room. The gravelled space takes the pressure off when there are larger parties and, being completely open, it's a lovely place to sit on sunny winter days.

Designer: Isabelle Greene

Above: *A big, grassy terrace is sheltered by the house and partly shaded by an enormous evergreen tree. In the cooler months, it is possible to enjoy the sun by sitting up this end but when the summer comes activities occur in the shade of the tree. This terrace is big enough to accommodate very large gatherings but loses out on intimacy because of its size.*

Paving vs Grass

Which is best?

- *Hard paving is the best surface for places where people congregate.*
- *It provides a level, firm footing which will not wear out.*
- *It may be used immediately after rain whereas grass may remain squelchy for a day or two and traffic will then damage the grass and compact the soil beneath.*
- *Furniture legs will sink into soft soil and, if wooden furniture is left permanently on grass, the dampness will rot the legs.*
- *Paving is clean and will not lead to muddy footprints in the house.*

Right: Although backed by shrubs and the neighbour's trees, this area has no shade until late afternoon. A deciduous vine over the pergola would change that, enclosing the space beneath and making it more intimate. Note the pleasant proportions of this structure; the timbers used are big and solid, not thin and flimsy.

Good Vine for Pergolas

In cooler climates, grapevines are the best choice for pergolas; they're fast-growing, deciduous, fairly hardy and you can eat the fruit or leave it for the birds. There are also purely ornamental varieties which do not produce much in the way of fruit but colour well in autumn. If your pergola has a western aspect, as here, shelter yourself from hot afternoon sun by stringing stout wires between the uprights and training the vine along them.

Places Separate from the House

Elaborate and simple solutions

A site away from the house may be more suitable and although we always recommend paving, whether you also build a structure such as a pergola is up to you.

A pergola can be decorative in itself, an alluring feature that will define and formalise the area. By growing a vine over it, you can quickly turn an open, sunny space into a shady, sheltered room; cool and comfortable in even the strongest sunlight.

A pergola may seem out of place in a wild, informal garden unless designed sensitively and with an eye to its impact on the surroundings. An alternative is to pave an area under a copse of trees and put a table and chairs there. Trees are nature's air-conditioners and the shade they cast will always be cooler than that cast by an umbrella or other artifical means. This is because leaves emit moisture, cooling the air as the moisture evaporates.

Left: Placing a table and chairs under a tree is the simplest way to create an area for outdoor living and if you don't go in for a lot of alfresco dining, this may be all you need. You should still pave the area under the table, laying enough for easy access around the furniture. If you find you are using the area more, pave the path to it as this will give it the importance it deserves and make access easier.

Left: Walls of dense shrubs and a ceiling of low branches create a cool atmosphere a few steps from the house. You may have a spot like this already; a very shady part of the garden where nothing much will grow. If so, consider its conversion into a people place. You may have to prune some low branches to raise the ceiling and cut an entrance but if it creates a roomy space, you've done well! All that's left to do is lay the paving.

Mystery and Intrigue

They're What Makes a Garden Secret

Built decades ago when gardens were more functional than ornamental, this old aviary and chicken house (still in use) was not meant to be a decorative feature but, over the years as the garden has matured, the overgrown building has acquired a charm of its own and become a point of interest in the garden. If an old building exists in your garden, consider its possibilites as a decorative ruin or, if sound, a storage space before you demolish it.

Concealment rather than openness is what sets a secret garden apart; you can't see into it from outside and, once inside, there are hidden parts that have to be explored. If you can conceal the boundaries of your property, its extent will remain a mystery to solve. If you can also hide neighbouring buildings but incorporate distant trees or outlooks, the garden will seem bigger.

A densely packed garden is intriguing and a little mysterious; it's so different from the usual landscape it stirs the curiosity of visitors.

Paths must be alluring and inviting, pulling you into the garden with a promise of something to see around the corner. Paths that plunge into dense shrubberies and then disappear around a corner will lure you no matter how many times you've been down them before.

Features, be they ornaments, artefacts or structures, increase the garden's curiosity value and make the landscape more diverse and stimulating.

A secret garden that has an air of mystery and intrigue will be an exciting place, visually rich and interesting no matter what the season. It won't demand the time and effort of a traditional garden with an immaculate lawn and rainbow beds of gaudy annuals. It's a different style of garden that appeals to private people and can be tailored to satisfy the enthusiastic gardener and the home-owner with wider interests that compete for time. Its attraction is the attraction of wild places.

The garden should be the main attraction; it should charm with its beauty and interest. Pleasing plant groupings will do this but artworks and ornaments can add another layer of appeal. Strategically placed, they can lead us from one section to another. This is the artist's own garden, a landscape of strange things; even the plants are oddly shaped and the effect works. For a more conventional garden you could restrict yourself to a few well-placed pieces and let the plants and their layout do the talking.

Above: This courtyard has some unusual structures which give it visual interest and a strong sense of the unexpected. First, there's an internal wall which creates a separate car space and hides the vehicle from the view of the main garden. That there's a wall dividing the garden into sections is curious enough but with its rough, adobe-like texture and earthy paint job, it acquires extra appeal, even a history. The gate, doorframe and rough-cut, vine-clad timbers above suggest an intriguing past but they're only a few years old. Forethought and planning have created the opposite impression. Through the gate, in the main garden, the lath-covered wall also looks like some crumbling building. It makes an attractive backdrop for the plants and adds to the garden's feeling of age.

Rodney Hyett

Left: What could be more intriguing than a path like this? The arch of foliage is the doorway to discovery. Who wouldn't head straight through the cave to investigate the sunny garden beyond?

Paths that wind through dense plantings to secluded clearings give secret gardens their mystery. It's possible to achieve this in quite small gardens if you are aware of how much space you have and what will fit within it. Then visualise the mature trees and shrubs in your garden, give them time and space to grow and you will create an alluring garden.

Index